The 2nd Time Around

*How a 2-Time Breast Cancer Survivor
Turned Pain into Purpose*

Shalana Teresé

Copyright © 2018 Nuance Publishing

All rights reserved. No part of this book may be reproduced or transmitted in any form or by any means, electronic or mechanical, including photocopying, recording or by any information storage and retrieval system, without written permission from the author, except for the inclusion of brief quotations in a review.

ISBN-13: 978-0692161104
ISBN-10: 0692161104
Printed in the United States of America

Table of Contents

Introduction v

Chapter 1
   Wandering Through the Wilderness 1

Chapter 2
   The Move 9

Chapter 3
   Ms. Wilhelmina 19

Chapter 4
   The Rush Back to TEXAS 35

Chapter 5
   Becoming the Widow 47

Chapter 6
   Torture and Nightmares 67

Chapter 7
   God Equipping You for the TASK! 73

Chapter 8
   The 2nd Time Around 77

Chapter 9
   The First Angel Visit 83

The 2nd Time Around

Chapter 10
    The California Hospital Visit.. 91

Chapter 11
    After the Holidays... 97

Chapter 12
    The Healing Zone! 105

Introduction

The 2nd Time Around was written on faith-based principles with the intentions to help catapult your thinking to the next level. It is to encourage and inspire you to understand that you too, have a God Driven Purpose!

One of my favorite passages from the book *Think and Grow Rich* by Napoleon Hill is, "Whatever the mind of a man can conceive and BELIEVE, IT CAN ACHIEVE!" It's one of the books that was introduced to me after the passing of my husband and is said to have been read by the phenomenal Oprah Winfrey eight times before she became wealthy. I imagined, if it took her eight times to get it, how many times will it take you? The Bible says in Deuteronomy 8:18, "But thou shalt remember the Lord thy God: for it is HE that giveth thee POWER to get WEALTH!" Now God says, He wishes that we prosper, even as our SOULS PROSPER! Anything and everything we need, we have full access. God's intentions are that we experience the finer things in life, and not live in lack.

This book is a message within itself, to remind the people that GOD STILL HEALS! Healing does not have to be singled out to any specific disease. There are other attributes of healings besides diseases. When the body

The 2nd Time Around

becomes UNEASED, it EXPERIENCES DISEASE! We are living in a world where the economic cancers of life are running rampant in households, marriages, relationships, children, and in our mental stability.

God said He wished that we would do a GREATER WORK! Imagine that! We have work to do! Please enjoy this book as it was written with LOVE, and was written to remind you that you too can use your life challenges and turn your Pain into Purpose! Enjoy!

Chapter 1

Wandering Through the Wilderness

It was so dark, a dark feeling. A feeling that is indescribable, but dark comes to mind. It was three months after my husband passed away. I was sitting in the Doctor's office and was told "Yeah, this is breast cancer." I didn't hear it, but then again, I did hear it. So that saying, "You see your life flash right before your eyes." Yep, that is what I felt in that very moment. "So, what does that mean exactly?" I asked. "Well, first, I apologize about your husband, but you have breast cancer," the doctor responded. I remember the room being dark. I felt like I was in a nightmare. Clearly, this is a mistake! What in the world could have possibly went wrong? "So, what does that mean exactly?" I asked a second time. "Well, you are going to need to have a double mastectomy, along with reconstructive surgery." I was in complete silence only to find out that the reconstruction was a series of surgeries, and not just one.

The 2nd Time Around

I couldn't think straight. However, I tried to cover my devastation, because clearly God wouldn't allow me to experience something as tragic as this; especially after my husband just passed. So as fast as my mind could think, what do I say in return? "Ohhhhh-Okay... so you are going to give me a boob job?" I asked. I was told that now was not the time to crack jokes, but he liked my style. "What does this mastectomy mean?" I asked again. Hopefully, to gain clarity this time. "Well, we are going to take your breasts, I suggest both, only because you just want them done at the same time." Boy, I wish I knew then what I know now. What was I thinking? What are my options? What do I do? Shoot, absolutely no time to think. He continued, "Then, we are going to expand your breasts by giving you tissue expanders, along with monthly injections. We also will reconstruct your nipple and areola area, finalizing your tattoos for the areola, for the 3-dimensional look." Good grief! Well, I have a headache now thinking about all these EXTRAS! It was Mother's Day weekend, May 5, 2010... yeah, you guessed it, it was surgery time.

I endured a five-hour surgery that consisted of removing the CANCER, my lymph nodes on my left side, and the start of reconstruction. My breast surgeon did her part, and my plastic surgeon followed behind her. Afterward, I heard the nurse calling my name. But once I opened my eyes, I couldn't see anything. My vision was blurry! Imagine that! SUPER SCARY! I could only see the silhouette of the person. "Stay calm, Shalana. You are going to be fine!" Well, at least that's what I kept telling myself. The moment was so horrific, and just so suddenly. I was the girl people would consider to be kind of bougie. I shopped at the finest grocery stores, took my prenatal vitamins, along with many other herbs thinking that I was doing myself and my family a favor. I was the wife who cooked meals, and shopped at Whole Foods and Sprouts, which are my favorites, and I remember asking my doctor, "What did I do wrong?" His reply was, "Absolutely nothing. This is just part of your story." "Some story." I thought to myself.

I can't even begin to tell you how painful all of this was. Literally the thought of it all makes the hairs stand on my arms and the back of my neck. The pains after that surgery I wouldn't even wish on my worst enemy. Although, hopefully, I don't have any of those. After my surgery, the breast surgeon came to check on me. She told me something very critical in terms of the movement of my journey! "Shalana, I must admit, I didn't think your surgery would go this well. I was expecting different." She said. "We did have to take your lymph nodes on your left side, and we tested your margins. Your margins on your left and your right were clear! NO CANCER!" I shut my eyes and immediately started REJOICING! Tears started rolling down my face. I was so happy. I felt the presence of God and I was so glad He gave me a testimony. As far as my body, it felt different. Not just different, but I no longer had breasts. Man, that was a hard pill to swallow! I was so scared to look down because I knew my breasts were no longer there. I looked eventually, but kind of at a glance, only to see my hospital gown was super flat; and I remember the anxiety kicking in. When my husband passed, I started having anxiety attacks. It was so sad because once they start, you must wait for them to pass. My experience with them were no walk in the park. Literally the room would start spinning and the walls seemed like they were caving in on me at the same time. I remember asking my doctor about it and telling him about this experience. That's when he shared with me that I was prone to those attacks. I also remember thinking, "Am I less of a woman now? Who would want to be with me in these conditions?" I remember thinking all sorts of crazy things that would take your mind into a dark place. But instead, the tears flowed on my smooth skin and instead of allowing my mind to go there, I REJOICED with gratitude! Gratitude that I was ALIVE! Gratitude that I was graced with a SECOND CHANCE! One thing for sure is that you MUST ALWAYS SPEAK LIFE over ANY SITUATION you may be FACING! I don't care what it looks like. It can seem as if death is knocking on the door, but you MUST KEEP YOUR FAITH! I ALWAYS speak over myself, my healing, my wholeness, and just the simple fact that God is a PRESERVER! When I first met my breast surgeon, we talked about options, etc. She talked about how I would more than likely be on chemo after the surgery. Well, clearly none of this made sense because why would we have that as an option when I didn't have the type that required chemo. So why on earth would I agree to that? I stuck to my FAITH! Yeah, it can save your life!

Wandering Through the Wilderness

There were times when I thought I was going to lose my mind! The nightmares, the night sweats, the horrific feeling of my husband being gone, the explaining to my children, the depression, the action on, action off effect. MY WORLD WAS IN COMPLETE TURMOIL! At least that's what it felt like. I have to say it; the WORD OF God is what kept me from literally snapping! If I didn't know of HIM, if I didn't have a relationship with HIM (GOD), believe me, I would have thrown in the towel by now. When the breast specialist was talking to me, I literally tuned him out. I referenced myself like the woman with the issue of blood. You know the story in the bible, right? I encourage you, if you haven't heard about her, trust me, at least read the story once! I like to reference the NKJV (New King James Version) St. Mark 5: 25-34. Isn't it amazing how we have no idea this woman's name, but we just know her as THE WOMAN WITH THE ISSUE OF BLOOD? I could relate to her. I had to remind myself, like the woman with the issue of blood, if I could just GET TO GOD! That's what I kept saying repeatedly. The bible says, that the woman knew if she could just get to Jesus (well close enough to HIM to touch the hem of his garment, she knew she would be made WHOLE! See, it was her FAITH THAT MADE HER WHOLE! FAITH, FAITH, FAITH! FAITH–the substance of things hoped for, the evidence of things not seen. (Hebrews 11:1)

Well, I had to implement that for myself. I'd just lost my husband, three months prior to all of this, honestly, everything was a blur. I literally had no time to think, SO I HAD TO HOLD ON TO MY FAITH! FAITH IN

The 2nd Time Around

KNOWING, FAITH IN BELIEVING AND FAITH IN PROSPERING! Yep, you guessed it. I will cover all of those. I know those are the three strategies as to partly why I'm still alive today. Oh boy, but the journey continues...

Wandering in the wilderness was no fun. I knew God, I loved God, I honored God, but I got to a point in my life after the five hours of surgery, and the four reconstructions, I felt as though I was just existing and not living. Remember the action on, action off effect? Well, that's just what it was. I knew I was gifted, I knew God had blessed me with his anointing, so if I was asked to pray, I prayed. It was effective. If I was asked to sing, I sang. Even if I could barely get the words out before completely losing it in the choir stand. Action on, carrying on in life as if everything was fine. Cancer was gone, but there was sooooo much more underlying that I WAS DEALING WITH! Action off, well let me give you an example. One time, and I remember this so vividly, I took my kids to school as I normally do. When I returned home, I started crying. I was in the corner, I dried up my face, and that's all I remember. Once I came to myself, it was 3:15 pm. What in the world just happened? I was there, literally all day, and I didn't budge. I was dazed and afraid! ACTION OFF! I started therapy and was told I had some type of condition which caused me to replay the incident over and over of my husband's passing. It had me depressed, because I relived that moment quite frequently. I started seeking all kinds of help, because clearly the therapist had some validity in what she was saying. But at any moment, I FELT LIKE I WAS GOING TO SNAP! I prayed to God to get me out of this feeling. I needed a change of environment, I wanted to GET AWAY! Although I moved out of the house where my husband had fell, every time I walked into the kitchen, I relived that tragic moment.

Chapter 2

The Move

School was out and we were all packed up and ready to move. I was willing to give up EVERYTHING to keep my SANITY. Trust me, and I was up for losing a lot. In terms of walking away from everything, that is. My home was GORGEOUS, I owned more than one vehicle, I had a wonderful church family, who I know LOVED me and my children, and supported me in any way they could. I was grateful for all of it and all of them but hear me out! Warning ALWAYS comes before destruction. Me losing my husband was an assignment all by itself to make me lose my mind. I'm telling you, I WAS ABOUT TO LOSE IT! I felt trapped and I knew if I didn't make a change quickly, I was going to SNAP! Have you caught on to how many times I said I was about to SNAP? Now what does that all entail? Honestly, I have no idea... but I know it wasn't good. I loved my kids dearly and I was determined to live, but there was something taunting me to the point where I was losing my sanity. So, off to

The 2nd Time Around

Virginia we go! Not everyone was on board with my decision, but it was TIME TO GO!

In the process of me living in Virginia, let me just say, that was the ABSOLUTE WORST EXPERIENCE in my LIFE! I DID NOT LIKE THAT PLACE. Now granted, the state itself has some wonderful people there! Oh, and my Bishop's Church, THE ABSOLUTE BEST! So, don't get me wrong, THE PEOPLE were GREAT. It was the EXPERIENCE that didn't seem to go in my FAVOR. Or at least that's how I felt. I could run down this and that and that and this, but the bottom line is it was a FAITH MOVE! And God asked me so clearly during different courses of events "DO YOU TRUST ME?" I had the feeling that something crazy would happen, but I had NOOOOOO IDEA it would be as drastic as it was!

We moved into a small town called Ruther Glen. I had a townhouse; three bedrooms, 2 and a half baths, 1800 square feet for $1200.00 a month. Man, those numbers sound good right about now. I'm currently residing in California, so you do the math! Anyway, the place was brand new and we were the first to live in it. I met with my mentor and coach by the way of telephone, (who lived in Philadelphia at the time) and I put my head down and built a business. I had the largest growing team within that organization and was on a roll. I loved my team, THE DREAM TEAM that is, and I loved the hope of flourishing in business. I didn't just talk the talk, but I walked the walk. I didn't require or expect anyone to do anything that I didn't do myself! And that was BUILD!

The Move

So, you know how you move and it takes some time for your mail to catch up? Well, when I received my mail, I received a letter that indicated that my income was going to be cut off effective June 1st. That's the day we left to move to Virginia and I had no clue. But, why? I had a letter from my employer that indicated my income would run for 36 months. Well at that time, we had barely passed a year, so something was wrong. How will I survive? What am I going to do? I have 3 kids and effective NOW, I will no longer receive any more of that income! HERE WE GO! I KEPT BUILDING, I kept encouraging, I kept pushing through the pain! I just kept going and going and going! Needless to say, I did have money saved, but it only lasted for so long. I was able to maintain the household for 5 months, and we got evicted. I mean it was no mercy, the judge wouldn't even listen to me. He didn't read the letter from my employer which ended up becoming long-term disability, and to top it off he didn't even give me 30 days to figure things out. He gave me 15 days! Matter of fact, he wouldn't even let me speak. HEARTLESS! And I will just leave it at that.

We were on the street. Driving from hotel to hotel, staying here and there, and guess what, YEP, I KEPT BUILDING. I would do my team calls sitting in the car outside of the hotel rooms before closing out for the night! Man, when I tell you I'm blessed! My girls continuously stayed on the honor roll and received awards. And my son, man he picked up so much slack. Think about it? Who do you think moved our stuff? It's only so much weight I could pick up, although there were times my son would tell me "MOM! Put that down! You are going to hurt your ninnies!!!" He was referring to my breasts. That's what we call them in my household. He would encourage me and remind me that GOD LOVES ME and that GOD is not going to ALLOW the devil to KILL ME! Isn't that something? He wasn't the straight A student, he dealt with dyslexia, and Irlen. Although dyslexia is common verbiage, Irlen may sound unfamiliar. Irlen is referred to as a processing disorder. It's not an optical issue, however, the brain's ability to process visual information is challenging. Homework with Tyion would take hours. As he got older he was able to explain what he saw when he would attempt to read. When he would read, the words would move, and he would have to wait for them to stop moving in order to read what the word(s) would say. This would then in turn cause delay in reading and comprehensions. One of my professors in college helped me in terms with dealing and coping with the two. He taught me that it's not a disorder, but my son had a GIFT! He also told me to never treat him like he has a disorder, never YELL when trying to get him to comprehend homework, assignments, etc., and always remind him how brilliant he is!!!! I must say, it has worked over the course of the years. There were several computer-based tests that I took that showed me exactly how my son along with probably millions of others out there, see things. Still, at my lowest points of my life, he encouraged me the most! We didn't have Hampton anymore, so things that he was concerned with as a child, he shouldn't have been. But he became the protector of myself and his sisters. One time he wrote me

The Move

a letter, and to this day it still encourages me to keep PUSHING through the PAIN! The letter came at the most perfect time. It was the time when I felt like such a failure, not having a place to stay or to call home other than this hotel, but when I tell you, it helped ME LIVE! In the most critical hours of my life, my son encouraged me to the point of borrowing HIS FAITH. He still believed in me although we were going from pillar to post. I guess he is just gifted in that manner. Tyion knew his mommy was going to pull through! Gosh I love my SON! I treat my kids with respect. I'm blessed to have them, because truly they are a gift from God and I know they honor me because of it. Proverbs 31:28 says, "Her children arise up, and call her Blessed; and her husband also, and he praiseth her." I'm honest with them, even though at times the conversations may have been difficult, and, they see I have developed a level of CONSISTENCY about building their WEALTH. It's an even trade. I know my babies love me and with their little innocent prayers, GOD kept me!

So, back to the hotel! My son has asthma, so I couldn't just stay anywhere. I had to be in a smoke free environment and at this point, now I've survived breast cancer. So once again, we just can't stay anywhere. I remember I was at my wits end. We were in a hotel all week, plus food, and you know what I don't know how, but money was always available, only GOD! Whatever I had, man it seems like he stretched it into thousands of dollars. This one day I was down to like my last couple hundred dollars, and all the hotels we were passing were over $100.00 per night. We kept driving and came across

The 2nd Time Around

this one hotel and you could tell it wasn't going to be cheap. My son was like, "Mom, try that one!" Now mind you, this hotel was sitting on a hill in Ashland, Virginia. I said, "No, Son. It's going to cost too much!" He replied, "Mom, you must go check." We were driving around, just roaming in the wilderness at this point for at least an hour and a half. We needed baths and were extremely tired. With tears in my eyes, I pulled up and walked in. I asked the lady behind the counter, "How much is it for the night?" and she told me $119.00 (you know that didn't include tax). I put my head down. "Thank you" I said and proceeded to walk away. Before I got to the door, she said "Well, how much can you pay?" I told her that I couldn't go over $100 at this point. I'm calculating in my head that I still must drive my kids to and from school which was a 30 min ride one way, and I still must feed them. She responded, "The lowest I could go is $109.00 so that's basically taking away the tax." I walked away and got back in the car. "So, we can stay?" My son asked. With tears in my eyes, I looked at him defeated, and shook my head no. Immediately, my son was like, "No, Mom. We have nowhere to go. Please go talk to her!" TEARS AGAIN! Now I can't control them. I went back inside and I asked the lady if there was anything she could do. "Do you have a promotion, a coupon, something?" She thought about it for a moment and said, "You know what? I can do it for $90.00. How does that sound?" "PERFECT! I will take it." I said. My face lit up and I was feeling somewhat hopeful! She looked at me and said, "Ma'am, please don't cry. Everything is going to be alright." I don't remember the name of the hotel, but it

The Move

had an actual library where you can check out books, in which I was glad to see that my girls each got a book after all that! It had a spiral staircase, very elegant, and it served breakfast in the morning. So, the good thing was I didn't have to spend money on breakfast. That was a HUGE plus for me. We all took showers and lights out.

The morning came. We are scrounging and I'm trying to calculate through GPS how long will it take to get my kids to school. A whopping 35 MINUTES! Now I can't find the brush! If you know us, our hair is too thick to be losing a brush! Sheeesh can anything else go wrong? I know a brush is like $5.00, but that $5.00 felt like $500.00. I held back the tears, but I felt it. I felt my breaking point coming. It was getting harder and harder to hold my tears back by the second. I'm talking to myself in my mind. "Shalana, please don't break down in front of all these strangers in this breakfast area." Then my mind went there! How in the world do you have an MBA, three kids and you are HOMELESS? Yes, you guessed it. Reality set in and hit me like a TON of bricks! I told my kids to help themselves and to even get extras for later. This IS SO UNFAIR I thought. I only tried to be obedient. Yes, I did ask God to do something and I needed a different environment. I needed to heal from all the turmoil, but am I willing to say I would have been disobedient if I knew all this was going to happen? Absolutely not! I would have NEVER left the comfort of my beautiful home, the life I built in the great state of Texas, if I thought all this was going to occur. But that was not the case. Spiritually, it was an assignment. Good gracious, what have I gotten myself into? I thought to myself. It was a complete and utter MESS! My son was talking about wanting to play football for Virginia Tech, so another thing was I figured if I'm already there, it would just be much easier college wise. Well, it didn't work out that way. The assignment had NOTHING to do with him attending college in Virginia.

With tears in my eyes, this lady comes from the back and she asks (in her pleasant singing voice) "Who wants waffles?" All three of my children responded in unison, "MEEEEEEEEEEE!" So of course, I put my head down and stood up, because now the tears are falling. She really didn't look at me, but she said, "Oh baby, I got it." So, I sat back down. The whole time with my head down, not making eye contact with her. After she finished the waffles, she came over to me and she held my hand. And in that moment, I felt the presence of GOD hovering over us. She looked me straight into my eyes and said, "You know the spirit knows the spirit, don't ya?" I said, "Yes ma'am" trying to respond as if I have manners. She said, "You have nowhere else to stay, do you?" I said, "No ma'am" while my lips were trembling. "And you're just about out of all your money, aren't you?" "Yes, ma'am" I said again. By this time, I was crying uncontrollably. The cry was hard, not loud, but gosh, this burden was heavy. She then told me when she walked into the room, that the Lord had already instructed her to help me. She said, "So you will not be homeless and you will have a place to stay." What a sigh of relief! I didn't know anything about this woman, and vice versa, but her presence was just

The Move

what I needed in that very moment. She told me that she had a friend who had a brand-new house and that she lived by herself. She was just returning from Africa (I believe it was a trip through the church), so she would ask her what she thought about us staying with her. If for some reason her friend were to say no, she expressed to me that she herself was married, her daughter lived with her and her house was small, but she ASSURED ME we will make it work. This lady was INCREDIBLE; to hear the voice of God in that instant, and to ACT IN FAITH! I will never forget that MIRACULOUS MOMENT! That specific conversation, once again, refueled my FAITH! Because I knew God heard my prayers, I was even more so convinced he saw my tears and sent HELP! The bible says, "The Lord will never put more on you than you can bear." And believe you me, I know this to be true! My God once again, came right on time for us! What manner of man is this the winds they obey? Matthew 8:27says, "But the men marveled, saying, what manner of man is this, that the winds and the sea obey him!" He's the GREAT ONE, that created the heavens and the earth. God can do just what HE wants! GOD IS IN CONTROL!

Chapter 3

Ms. Wilhelmina

My emotions were everywhere, however, everything was set up. I was going to meet the lady after I got back from dropping off the kids. I told the lady what room number I was in, and she said they would come knock on my door at 1pm. Knock, knock, knock! I looked through the peep hole and two ladies were standing there. One in which told me she would be back. I opened the door, nervous and embarrassed all at the same time. "Baby, what's your name again?" "Shalana," I replied. "Well this is Ms. Wilhelmina." She said. The lady looks at me and says, "Nice to meet you." "Thank you," I said, "Nice to meet you too!" She literally looked at me from the top of my head down to my feet, paused and said, "She can stay." and proceeded to walk out the door. The other lady was so excited. I took a deep breath and said "Thank you!" So, the discussion went like this: "Baby listen, I must go get a MAMMO-GRAMMY (too cute), and I will be home later." I'm quite sure she meant mammogram. "Better yet, let's go to my house now, so she will know where I live, and that way after school, she can go get her kids and go straight to the house." I followed them...

We pull up to two acres of land, all rock, no grass, beautiful home sitting right smack in the middle of nowhere! I get out the car, follow Ms. Wilhelmina in the house, and this is what happens... "Baby look, this is your son's room," She said. We then walk to another room. "And this room is for you and your girls. Your bathroom is over here, I don't use it, because I have my own. The towels are in this cabinet. Here is the kitchen, I hope you can cook, because I don't! Any questions?" "No," I responded. Her room was on the other side of the house. Still to this day I have NO idea what her room looks like, because quite frankly, I had no business in there. She had two living room areas, but one area. Of course, I just wouldn't let my kids in there for the sake of possibly messing something up. "I hope you guys feel safe. This is God's house and you all are welcomed. If you need anything, call me. Here's your keys and I will return later." She closes the door and she leaves. WOW! I stood there in AWE! A stranger opens her house to us and trust us; not making us feel uncomfortable but welcomed to the point of her leaving and saying she will be back later. Lord you are so awesome! I just had to give him some time and worship. Thanking him for keeping us all safe, making a way out of no way. Have you heard that term? Well, it's true. My back was up against the wall and I knew for sure in my Faith in Knowing, God provided.

Ms. Wilhelmina

I was so happy to go get my babies from school. I knew they were going to be happy to sleep comfortably, with no worries. So, once we got to the house, we took showers. I can't remember what we ate that day, but not too long after we just relaxed in comfort. This lady's home was SPOTLESS! Ahhh, the feeling on the inside, when someone shows you they genuinely care. This lady was one of a kind, and an absolute blessing. At times, I was like okay, when is she going to change? She never did. She kept me encouraged, she prayed for me and with me, she made sure that she handled us with care. What an amazing woman! As time passed, we were basically now like family. She never put a time frame on when we had to leave and quite honestly, I wish I had stayed longer. Well you know the saying, you don't want to wear out your welcome, but clearly in this case, that was not an issue. I know she would have nourished us more with love and filled us with the word of God. This woman in my eyes is an EXCELLENT human being; so, kind, gentle, and caring... truly God sent... her and of course, the lady who was obedient in helping my family get off the street.

One day while my kids were in school, people kept calling about my car payment. Remember the eviction? Well, I got behind on my payments also. Not that anything else could go wrong, but of course it did. I spoke with a gentleman this one specific day. I was very honest about the whole situation and told him, "Sir, I literally just moved myself and my children into a complete stranger's house. If you just give me till Friday, if I don't have an arrangement to get you all the money, I will tell you where I am." But honestly, I'm in the middle of nowhere. I don't even recall seeing a street name. Well of course I know there was one, but I really didn't know. He said, "Well get settled and call us back Friday." This was a Thursday. I took my kids to school, went on about my day, went and picked up my kids, and we were so tired, cause remember it's at least 35-40 minutes to get to our new place, from the school. Mentally, I was exhausted; trying to wrap my head around everything, just trying to keep it together. Got my kids, we walked in the house, my son was in the restroom, but he saw something outside the window. "Mom" he yelled. "Someone is taking our car!" By the time I got to the front door, I can see the repossession happening in that very second. I sat on the couch and I just cried. Lord, how? Why? How am I supposed to get my babies to school? It's way too far to walk, and we are literally in the middle of nowhere! My kids all piled on the couch next to me, and they started crying. This literally ripped me into pieces. I had no answers. It was getting dark, oh and one of the main factors here, is that I had absolutely NO service in her house. I couldn't make phone calls, go on internet, nothing. So, my son agreed to run with me as far as we could so that we can try to get reception. We are in Ashland, Virginia, or somewhere like that, and it's about 22 degrees. We ran, and it was a road and a bunch of trees. No sidewalk, just road, cars passing by, and when we made it to the end of the road, I was able to make the call. I called the police, so they could direct me to who had my car. There was a wait time to get information, and

Ms. Wilhelmina

yes, I'm worried sick. I left my girls in that house, so we started running back, a couple of times my foot fell into the bushes, and God only knows how creeped out I was. I had no idea what was in there, and to top it off its pitch black. No street lights and a very dangerous decision. It was at least two miles before we got back in the house and my throat was on fire! I was so exhausted, but at least I knew who to call. Now once everything sinks in, what in the world am I going to tell this lady? What would she think of me? Well, hopefully she won't notice. Well, of course she is! I just chuckled to myself. I shook my head and waited to see how this conversation was going to go. For starters, Ms. Wilhelmina was hardly ever home, like this lady solely trusted me with her house. Now she did come home every night, but when I tell you this lady worked the ministry, she was always out helping someone.

When she came home, she spoke to us, went and took her shower, and she came in the living room with us. She asked "Where's your car? In the shop?" OMGOSH, here we go. I was like you know what, to myself, just tell her the truth. I replied, "No, it was repossessed." She was like, "Really?" I thought she was going to start asking me a bunch of questions. I thought she was going to start drilling me on why it's important to have a car, especially way out in her neck of the woods, but you know what, she did the complete opposite. I will NEVER forget her response. She said, "Oh, well if they took that one, then that means God is going to bless you with another one! Let's put on some praise music!" she said excitedly. My mouth was wide open in awe, like really? Who treats people like this? Well, yeah you guessed it, Ms. Wilhelmina does. She walked to her music system, put some praise music on, and literally starting dancing in praise, and thanking God for my upcoming car. How phenomenal is this woman? I thought to myself! Well of course, right cause that's what God does. But she was so clear in knowing; her FAITH IN KNOWING that God was going to bless us. It was so crystal clear to her! This allowed me to borrow some of her faith! My babies joined in and we danced in praise, thanking God for what He was going to do. After turning down the music, we were just having general conversation, and she was like "Well you are going to have to take me to work in the morning." I looked at her in confusion. She said, "I must BE THERE at 6:20 A.M., so we can leave at 5:45 a.m." Still confused, she says, "Well you must take the babies to school, don't ya?" "Yes, ma'am." I replied. She said "And go to where your car is, because they will give you your possessions." Mind you, everyone had to use the rest room that day, so we all jumped out the car, left back packs, shoes, all our important documents, birth certificates, health insurance, you name it. "Just do what you must do and come pick me up later!" She said. Could this lady get any better? I mean, WOW! The tears became tears of Joy, and my babies were smiling. We ended the night happy and thankful!

The holidays were approaching, Thanksgiving to be exact. She indicated that we could have dinner with her family, and that we were going to have a glorious time! I felt at

Ms. Wilhelmina

ease, but still sometimes there was a part of me that felt so helpless. I felt like such a failure, but God knew exactly what I needed to be built up and not torn down. This phenomenal woman of God had four children who were all grown. Her daughter and husband had a beautiful home and we all fellowshipped there for the holiday. Then Sunday was approaching, and she asked me to go to church with her, and I agreed; we had such a glorious time. This church was huge, had a coffee shop, book store, a children/youth church, their own gymnasium, and it was all dominations. I sat in awe watching all colors of life, glorifying and praising God! Everyone there seemed so nice and we had such a great time. The "other lady" attended the church as well. Her daughter from what I remember was not there, but I was able to meet her husband. Just all around GREAT PEOPLE!

The time was approaching for me to get my apartment. I was moving in on December 5th. I remember that day, because that's my best friend's birthday from when I lived in Germany. She's a twin, and every year I think of them. Once again, I was reminded that we didn't have to move, and quite frankly, it's just now registering what she was saying. The place I got was... well let's just say it wasn't something my kids nor I were used to. The rent was cheaper, $960 a month, so from $1200.00, I felt like I could make it work. The whole townhouse had been remolded, granite in the kitchen, hardwood floors, the works. Ms. Wilhelmina's son in law helped me move. Now we were in our place, but for some reason, I could tell Ms. Wilhelmina was not too happy. I mean after all the love and expressions she gave us while being at her home, it was just strange that now she didn't show that same level of energy. What is it? I thought. Well, she didn't really say anything to me, but once I found out why her excitement was diminished to almost nothing, IT WAS TOO LATE!

The house didn't feel right. I couldn't sleep, I felt uneasy. My kids couldn't sleep, something was just not right. My son woke up and his arm was red, but to have a son whom is allergic to many things, and have asthma, it didn't seem suspicious to me. However, it seemed like every day that passed, one of us woke up with red marks. Around the third night we were there, we woke up and Tyion's whole arm was literally showing blood! What in the world? This is too much. It got to the point that now my girls have bites all over them and the one episode that really took the cake, my youngest daughter had a piece of meat missing from being bit on her back. I was furious! Oh, and not to mention one morning I woke up and I had blood on my face! Pretty gruesome, huh? Well imagine how WE felt! WE did not sleep at all. We were afraid to, because now we figured out that this townhouse was INFESTED with bedbugs. They were EVERYWHERE and I didn't know anything about these little demons, but I tell you, it was just out of control! We went to the doctor, and I expressed to him what was going on. Side note: I used so many remedies and this and that, and even management claimed to do an evacuation of them, but guess what? It only lasted for a few days and they would come right back! I remember speaking to my cousin,

Ms. Wilhelmina

Audra. Man, that girl does not get enough credit for her knowledge. She told me, "Shalana, nothing is going to get rid of those BASTARDS!" I was HOLLERING LAUGHING but PISSED ALL AT THE SAME TIME! Okay, don't get all holy on me, I didn't say it, she did! Anyway, the bites were so bad that the doctor had to prescribe us medication. I remember showing someone at the church where we were attending. I can tell from her expression she knew we were in a bad place! I don't remember the doctor's name, but I asked him what I should do, because clearly, we can't live like this! He said, "Do you want me to be honest with you?" "Of course!" I replied. He said "LEAVE!" I was like we literally just got there by now we are in the middle of the month, and well you can imagine what had to be done to get this place being as though we were evicted! Just the thought of that word (evicted) makes me cringe! He said, "Shalana! LEAVE!" Sheeesshhhhhh, I felt like he was super serious! And guess what! I had informed Ms. Wilhelmina's son in law and daughter what we were experiencing and guess what? They all agreed. I don't know however, for the life of me, why I didn't ask if we could come back. Honestly, I wasn't trying to make the stay permanent, so I guess that's why I didn't even bother.

During this turmoil, you remember I didn't have a car, right? Well, the Sunday after I moved in, the daughter texted me and asked me if she could talk to me after church. My mind was racing, because I had no clue what she was going to say to me. Maybe I didn't pay her husband for helping me move, maybe she was upset that it was after 9 p.m. when we got everything done. I had no clue what this conversation was going to be about.

After the service, she called me. She told me that when her husband came home after helping us move, he was like "Honey, I must tell you something." I'm thinking ohhh boy-but I knew I did nothing wrong. So, I listened carefully to what she had to say! She told me that when her husband got home, he was like, "Honey, I must tell you something," and then she said, "No, wait I must tell you something." The husband said excitingly, "Let me go first!" The wife replied, "No, let me go first!" just as excited! And almost literally at the same time, they said, "We must give Shalana our van!" My mouth hit the floor!!!! Not only did her mother bless me more than I could ever imagine, by allowing myself and my three kids stay in her home, but now her daughter and son in law wants to GIVE me their vehicle? WHO DOES THAT? There was complete silence, except with her talking on the other line. "Hello, Hello," she said. "Ohhh uhhhh yes I'm here." "Shalana, did you hear what I said?" she asked? "Ummmmm yes I did," I replied. "But wait, I can't take your..." She cut me off and said, "Will you be home at 7?" Well of course I would, I thought to myself- I didn't have transportation. She said, "Okay see you then." and hung up the phone. I couldn't believe this. Despite what I endured, my babies getting bit at night, all of us waking up with blood on different parts of our bodies, man that's just GROSS, nevertheless, GOD STILL SHOWED UP! I wish I had photos to show how graphic these bites were, but back to the blessing! This van, was such a blessing,

Ms. Wilhelmina

cause now we must move again. It was so spacious and could literally fit up to 7 people, had the captain chairs, leather interior, and a tv/dvd player so the kids could watch movies. When I tell you right on time! Remember when I shared how when my car was repossessed, Ms. Wilhelmina praised God, for my new car, whelp, GOD did just that! What a Blessing!

We moved into that god-awful townhouse on December 5th, and by February, nothing still was done. I was fed up, my kids were agitated, and we all had enough. See when your peace is compromised, nothing else matters but to get it back! PEACE, PEACE, PEACE! I can't say enough about it. When the workers came out to inspect the home, I was so glad I was there. I remember that conversation so clear. One of the workers were on the phone, and HE YELLED "What do you mean the house is VACANT? I'm looking at the tenant and her face is BLEEDING from being bit!" He was so furious, because prior to that Christmas time, everyone was on their own scheduling and so we had to wait it out. The worker was so upset, because he said there is NO WAY we should be living there. He lifted the carpet in my son's room, and I wanted to puke! How did I get in this filth? Mind you, we were all piled up in my room, and for some reason they did not go in the living room, so my son would sleep on the couch. I went to management and I told her as of that Saturday, we would be gone. And as for February, I was not paying rent. The lady knew, because she never disputed it. Basically, I told her, "Don't come for me, and I won't come for you!" Although I had brand new furniture, I lost

The 2nd Time Around

everything, but I just wanted to get out of that house. I was so GLAD when that was over!!!!

We found a better place to live. A much better community, a bit pricy, but let's do it! Now I'm paying $1350 a month, but the apartment was spotless, and NO BED BUGS! But let's talk about initiating a self-help guide right about now!

Life happens, and the things you can't control, don't let them control you! That's what my late husband Elder Anthony Hampton told me! Man, he was one of a kind! RIP, Hampton!

Ms. Wilhelmina

Turning PAIN into PURPOSE Worksheet

Reflecting Moments:

Has there ever been a time when you felt like giving up? Let's reflect on that time, and jot down some things that you did to get yourself out of your STINKING THINKING! (you will thank my Coach Terence Smith for that one!)

_____
_____
_____
_____
_____
_____
_____
_____
_____
_____
_____
_____
_____
_____
_____
_____
_____
_____

The 2nd Time Around

Did you use any strategies of faith to get your mind set out of that circumstance? Would you say that your Faith is now stronger from that specific circumstance, based off the strategies you used?

_____
_____
_____
_____
_____
_____
_____
_____
_____
_____
_____
_____
_____
_____
_____

Let me be transparent... some occurrences in my life, were not as bad as the others. I've always believed myself to be strong. However, there were times when I just didn't know what to think. And that's when I had to implement my Faith in BELEIVING. See, when you are confused and discombobulated, that's not of God. So, whatever you are believing God for, know you must initiate your faith, God does not operate in confusion,

Ms. Wilhelmina

that's why it's so imperative that if you are going through something and there's confusion, you must gain clarity. You must feel a sense of peace within your inner self. Guidance, clarity, believing, and faith, they all coincide with each other. Faith is the substance of things hoped for and the evidence of things not seen. You can't see it, but you have faith in BELEIVING that it's there, or it can be obtained. Now let's take the tragedy of my husband passing if you will. You know the saying, I thought I was going to lose my mind, but God kept me? Well HE DID! Let me explain... the tragedies that I endured, especially the one with me losing my husband, it was gruesome. Those incidents were designed to KILL ME! LITERALLY! The bible says that the enemy comes to kill, steal and destroy! More specifically, the scripture reads: John 10:10, "The thief cometh not, but for to steal, and to kill, and to destroy: I am come that they might have life, and that they might have it more abundantly." And that is exactly what the enemy was trying to do, KILL ME OFF! But GOD BLOCKED IT!

Chapter 4

The Rush Back to TEXAS

I hate to say it, but it was time to go back to Texas. During my stay in Virginia, we were there for a year. The time was not very long, but it seemed like FOREVER! We had endured so much in Virginia; income being cut off, I broke out in hives, being evicted, being homeless going from hotel to hotel, car repossessed, bed bug infested townhouse, all resulted in me being UNEASED! My kids are my HEROS, because none of them EVER FOLDED! Of course, we cried, we laughed, and we tried to make the best of whatever situation we were in; but when I tell you, they are an absolute blessing. Even in the times when I know my faith was not at its highest level, I still had to faith *it*! I don't like the term "Fake it 'till you make it," but I definitely learned how to *faith it*! I'm not sure about you, but I hate the thought of even reliving those horrific moments.

The 2nd Time Around

One day, I felt a knot. Where in the world did this come from? It was weird and was on top of my left breast. At first, it was very small and although it wasn't very big, I knew something was odd. Once you learn your body, you will know how to identify certain things that are just not quite right. I set an appointment, and, I felt like a sacrifice. I felt like everything in that place was so diabolical, that I needed to get away as fast as I could. I know it seems a bit harsh but let me paint the picture. I went to the doctor and I was placed in this room that had a table that you lay on during your visit. However, the chair was sitting upright! The doctor informed me that the knot under my arm was a disease, and that the knot she saw, she was almost sure it was cancer! Well wait, I know a man that already healed me. I had a five-hour surgery, followed by reconstructive surgeries. My lymph nodes were removed on my left side, and I was informed that my margins on my right and left were negative. So how in the world could I be reliving this again, especially after my husband had passed away? It was October 2013, and I was told that the cancer has returned.

The doctor kept coming in and out of the room and she decided to do a biopsy. Gosh, the pain was brutal. She was literally digging and pulling pieces of the tumor. A nurse was in the room with her, but then other ladies kept coming in the room. The worst part of all this, is that ALL of the nurses gravitated towards me and were surrounding me. One nurse started rubbing my hands and telling me everything was going to be okay. I'm sure they didn't mean any harm, but these women already

The Rush Back to TEXAS

decided what was going to happen to me. Meanwhile, a different nurse on my other side started touching my hair, and I remember this so clearly, her words to me were, "Don't worry about your hair, it will grow back!" OOOOHHHHHHH NO! Anyone who know me, knows I take well care of my hair. It's my Glory for God's sake, and NO ONE will decide what happens to it except me. I realized, the darkness that was trying to lure me into the pit. Now I'm not saying that the nurses were dark, but this is what the enemy does when he's trying to lure you back into darkness. They were all nice and I'm sure they had good intentions. I knew they only wanted to console me the best way they knew how, and I'm also certain, because they were nurses, they were also trained to be a certain way. Once again, Lord, here I am! What should you have me to do? These nurses, including the doctor had already given me a diagnosis without even doing any type of procedures, testing, NOTHING! I felt like it was a trap. I expressed my concerns and how I do not agree with chemo, and that I don't like the way they were talking. The other thing that was so strange, is several of those women had breast cancer themselves, they told me! I didn't like that at all. WHY SO MANY OF THEM? I felt on edge the whole time I was there! I couldn't wait until that visit was over! Once I left, I knew that I would NEVER see those women again. I was on the search for another doctor. I found one, and she was a little less daunting. What I didn't understand about the first doctor I saw, is that she wasn't willing to set me up for surgery to remove the knot, which wasn't very big at all. I guess once she realized I was not returning, she would call me personally. She even offered to take a piece of the cancer, but not all of it! HUH? This was crazy! I was like no way, why would I go through surgery and you purposely leave cancer inside of me? Ummmm, no thank you I thought. I never returned the call.

The new doctor was not so bad. She was more compassionate to listening to what my concerns were, and what I was and was not willing to do. I asked her a specific question about her thoughts of me taking chemo, and she told me that the type of cancer I had didn't require chemo. Her exact words were, "It wouldn't do anything for you! You don't have the type that require chemo!" Such a sigh of relief! I felt like somebody had done their homework! Well, it's a start. About surgery, she too didn't want to do it right away; she wanted to wait six months! What in the world is wrong with these people? It bothered me. Why six months? No telling what could happen by then! Nah, I wasn't having it. What do I do?

In the meantime, I would consult with one of my good sister/friends and we would encourage each other. One day, we were on the phone and I could tell she was exhausted with just everything that was going on. She didn't tell me fully what was wrong, but I knew it wasn't anything good. She referred me to her holistic doctor in Texas, but he was so popular, people were flying in from all over the world, just to see him. You would have to put yourself on the waiting list, and based off how critical your condition was, if an opening came about then you would get a call. I set up everything and was placed on

The Rush Back to TEXAS

the list. However, I did tell them that I would need at least two weeks for traveling purposes. About two weeks later, I received a call that there had been a cancellation, and if I could come in that week on a Thursday, but then there was silence, and the young lady said, "Oh I apologize. You have a message here saying you live in Virginia." She then said she was going to see what she could do and call me back. I knew the time was going to be soon, so I just started checking flights. I asked my friend if I could stay with her while I was there in Texas for the treatments, and she agreed. The consultation was $150.00, and I knew the supplements depending on what was suggested, plus the cost of treatment was going to be a bit costly. I needed to allocate at least $500.00 to the side in addition to my flight! When you have children, you can't just think of yourself. Planning something like this takes a lot of designating and making sure your decisions are right.

I don't remember the exact date, but it was a week before Thanksgiving. I GOT THE CALL! I could go see Dr. Duncan, have my consultation, get my supplements, and hopefully get some treatments, and be back home by Thanksgiving. PERFECT!

When I walked into the facility, I felt such warmth. I knew the presence of God was in there. My consultation was full of emotions because Dr. Duncan knew things that I had not uttered to a soul! He carefully explained exactly what he does, and I could tell he was led by the Holy Spirit. Now, in that regard, how in the world did he know these things? Oh yeah, HOLY SPIRIT! The warm feeling in the facility, was exactly what I NEEDED. One of the things that stuck out was the soothing Christian/Gospel music. The staff were so pleasant and I felt so safe. Although my analysis was way more than expected, I knew I was at the right place at the right time.

My treatments started and I felt I was on my way to optimal health. I spoke healing over my body every day, no matter what I felt like. Dr. Duncan had prayed with me, we touched and agreed for my complete and total healing, he even offered deliverance, because man I tell ya, child hood things... hmmmpffff well that's another book.

The treatments that I received were so reviving, and that week went by so fast. I didn't want to leave. Once I returned to Virginia, I was talking with my kids, and my son asked, "Mom, when do you have to go back for treatment?" "In six weeks," I replied. And it was almost like unison, my kids said, "We should just go back to Texas!" OMGOOOOSHHHH! That's exactly what I wanted to hear. *Man, talk about out of the mouth of babes:* St. Matthew 12:16. Now I truly believe that everything happened for a reason. I started thinking about how I would get my family back to Texas, and if it was something I could pull off. I looked around the apartment, although it was new and clean, there was no furniture, other than my kids' beds. I managed to buy them a bed, but other than that, I slept on the floor. I had a blow-up mattress until one morning I woke up flat on the floor. It was funny and sad at the same time. Since I lost all my new furniture, it really wasn't a whole lot of stuff. My girls went to play, and I asked my son how soon did he think it would take for us to pack up and leave? I was determined to be in that environment in which I had experienced in Texas. From the look of things, we were there a little over a year and nothing was working out. In the natural sense I say that, however, spiritually my faith was tested, but honestly, I knew my level of faith was significantly increased.

I must admit, I saw more visions while living in Virginia than I ever had in my life! I truly believe and KNOW it was GOD assuring me that HE had me covered. I knew God's protection was over myself and my children. It was just going through the journey that was challenging. I often think that Virginia wouldn't have been half as bad, if I didn't lose my income, and if I didn't get there based off tragic incidents that occurred. But think about it, although those horrible occurrences happened, GOD was still in the midst. We were still blessed. We were ALIVE! Only through the grace of God, but you know what? I had my babies, and sometimes, you must allow people to go through their moment, because EVERYONE handles tragedies differently. Regardless to what people may have felt, if I didn't have the TEST, I would not have the TESTIMONY! Ahhhhhh thank GOD for the revelation. The bible says we overcome by the words of our testimonies! (paraphrasing—Rev. 12:11) So in essence, there is life in sharing what you went through and how God pulled you out!

The first week I moved to Virginia, my mom came down the following week. It was close to Father's Day, and we were sitting in the living room and she mentioned that Georgia wasn't too far, and since Father's Day was coming, we could go see Gren-daddy (that's what I call my grandfather). Shocked, I was thinking, now I know she can't be serious? I literally just drove over 20 something hours to get to Virginia, and Lord only knows, I DO NOT want to drive anywhere else!

She insisted, and by looking up the information, we were twelve hours away. So, my mom said we could do six and six, and be there in no time. I did indicate how TIRED I was, and although it did sound like a fantastic idea, I'll pass. Well, she wasn't having it. Funny thing is, that my mom did all that prepping and planning, and do you know she literally drove one hour, and basically slept the whole way there? Now I'm not talking about her, because we have laughed about this several times. But what I didn't share with her is this: I am bad with directions (well she knows that part all too well), and I truly feel that God communicated with me in such a way to elevate my faith even more! Now, my mom was sleep most of the way, so I was just conversing with God and praying as I'm driving. Now let me tell you my experience. I had asked God so many questions. I was also whining to God, as I often do, about this that and the other, and once I got quiet, I know the Lord was thinking: *if she would just listen, I will tell her what I'm doing.* I heard, "Do you trust me?" and I was really thinking to myself, duh, after all this, but humbly I replied, "Of course." Then God gave me the most precise analogy. He said, "You are using a GPS device to get you where you need to go. You really

The Rush Back to TEXAS

don't know if you are going in the right direction, yet you are trusting the fact that this small device, that you really don't have any clue, if it really works, that you will end up in Georgia. Now how is it that you will trust in something such as this, but you won't TRUST ME?" Dannnggggggg I thought. Just shut me down. So, in other words, you are trusting in manmade material things, but when I tell you something, then you want to ask me a bunch of questions as if I don't know what I'M DOING! AHHHH THEN IT HIT ME, THE Lord was directing me once again, and he was there with me all along just like this time, and the time before that, and the time before that. Man, how many times before that could I go? We will be here forever, HE'S just that GRACIOUS!

Now think of a time, when you know, you had to activate Your Faith in Knowing! Knowing that although you don't see your way, God pulled you through that very thing in which you thought was impossible!!!!!

The 2nd Time Around

Faith in Knowing

"There was a time when I experienced…" Jot down that experience. You will be able to reference it later when you need to be encouraged!

_____
_____
_____
_____
_____
_____
_____
_____
_____
_____
_____
_____
_____
_____
_____
_____
_____.

The trip to Georgia was awesome! It was so good to see and spend time with my grandfather (Gren-daddy)! We had a good time and I don't regret not one moment of it! My kids had a blast and everyone was just so happy! Now I must admit, on the way back, Pooch (my mom) did

The Rush Back to TEXAS

much better. She gave me about four hours of driving, so the return wasn't so bad after all.

Chapter 5

Becoming the Widow

N ow, let's go back to how this all started. Clearly, we haven't referenced this yet, because it's difficult to talk about. Over time it has gotten better, but truthfully, the hurt never goes away.

Life was great and my husband had relocated us to Texas in 2006. There was a married couple who were looking to sell their home! They had a five-bedroom house, play room, study room, two living rooms, two full baths and a half bathroom, a huge back yard, a fireplace, and the list goes on and on. The house was huge! 4,000 square feet to be exact and it was GORGEOUS! We were set and as I mentioned, life was great. My husband found us an awesome church home; Greater Love Chapel, Church of God in Christ, still under the leadership of Bishop Jimmy W. Glenn, Sr. and Sylvia Glenn. We had great leadership, the choir was the bomb, great movement, ministry was going well, and really you couldn't ask for much else. We adjusted well to the new state and it really didn't take much time. I think because of such a great welcome of the membership, it was easy to feel at home. We served the ministry, I sang in the choir, and my husband was an ordained Elder. I also was able to work in the finance department; which was easy for me because I was a financial analyst at my regular job. My degrees were both Bachelor of Science in Business Management, and a Master's in Business Administration, MBA.

Fast forward to August 2009. I was having some girls over, and I was hosting a candle party. We were having so much fun and my husband walked through the door. The girls spoke, and he did speak back, but it wasn't how he would normally do, and pick with the girls. He just said hello, he spoke to me personally, and then he said, "Excuse me," and went into our room. He shut the door.

My heart sank, because I knew something was wrong. When he walked in the door he was holding his neck, but I figured that it was from work stress and from driving. I told the girls to excuse me, and I went in the room. He was laying across the bed on his back, and I said silently with concern, and I felt my voice tremble. "Babe, are you okay?" I walked a couple steps closer. "Babe, what happened?" Taking more steps towards the bed, I said, "What is it?"

He looked at me and I saw fear! I know my husband! I really didn't know what to think. He kept looking at me, so I just stood there. I took his hand and I kissed it. Gosh, I could feel the pain. I just didn't know what it was. "Babe," I said once more, and then he started talking. He

Becoming the Widow

said, "Babe, my neck hurts badly! So bad to the point where it was affecting my walking. I could barely lift my feet at work." He was the manager, but he said someone was concerned, and the VP called him and told him to go home. He said he had been dragging his feet all day, because for some reason it was hard for him to walk regularly. I felt a big knot in my throat. I took a deep breath and I told him I would call the doctor. I also told him that I would tell the girls to go home so that we could have quiet time. Of course, he didn't want me to do that. He said he was going to take a bath, eat, and then go to bed. He told me to feel his neck and I felt two knots on it. He explained that's what was hurting him. I asked him what it was and obviously, he didn't know either. I finished my party, and of course by the time I went into the room, he was fast asleep. I kissed him on his cheek. He said, "I LOVE YOU" and turned over. I had tears in my eyes, because I really didn't know what to do. Hampton was my strong man, he protected me, and to see him hurting was too much for me!

After my husband had his doctor appointment, our conversations were very uncomfortable. He told me that the doctor indicated that he was going to run tests, but he was almost CERTAIN it was cancer! Literally, those words went straight out the window. HOW? I thought. WHY?

"Babe, he doesn't know for sure. Let's wait 'till the reports come back." I said eagerly. By September, my husband was already scheduled for chemo. Everything was just going so fast. Stage 3, as they call it. The tumor on his neck, that thing was mad, and it kept getting bigger and bigger! Gosh that's not fair, but it was his decision and he decided to take it.

Meanwhile, I constantly prayed for my husband, but you know what? I had to have a secret prayer for myself. See one Sunday afternoon, my first lady preached a message. In the message, she indicated how the doctors told her she had breast cancer, and that she was going to have a mastectomy, and on and on. But at the end of the message, when she went back to the doctor, they couldn't find anything! GLORRRYYYYY TO GOD! That's awesome! RIGHT? Well, my husband and I was talking about it, and I referenced her message and how she preached a powerful word. I remember so clearly. I said, "Man, you just never know." While I was rubbing my breast at the same time, and I paused, and felt again, and I promise I felt something, but I felt like I was being a bit paranoid. After the third time of me rubbing, I was like "Babe, feel this." He looked at me. "NO BABE! There's nothing wrong with you." I said "No, babe, for real. Please feel." He felt my left breast, and he said, "Well maybe you should go to the doctor." I never got a chance to. Hampton's neck was hurting and before I knew it, he was on chemo. So what time did I have to go to the doctor?

Dear Lord,

I don't know what's going on, but I felt something in my breast. So, until we get Hampton better, can you please

Becoming the Widow

JUST HOLD ME OVER, and then I will see what's going on.

Simple, short, and sweet. I truly had to ask God to cover me, because I really didn't get to think about myself. My life was all over the place. My husband would have chemo for four hours, I had three children who needed to go to school, and then after all that I would go to work! I remember one of the ministers offered his time to sit with my husband on more than one occasion. I specifically remember being told, "Sis. Hampton, I would go to encourage your husband, and Hampton would end up encouraging me." WOW, that speaks volumes. Sometimes, it just takes a little time to let individuals know you care about them. A lot of the burdens were carried by the members of the church. Man, I tell you, I knew when they were praying for us…I could feel it.

My husband was transferred to Baylor Hospital in Dallas. That was 51 miles one way from my house. I would literally pick up my kids after work, feed them dinner, and put them to bed. Often, I would let Tyion know I was leaving, lock all the doors, praying cause clearly, I can't take them with me, they have school in the morning, it was just a lot. I would pray the whole way there. Even if I only saw Hampton for an hour, he always wanted me back on the road before midnight. I would go. I would do ANYTHING for my husband, absolutely anything! I was tired and overwhelmed. The back and forth really put a toll on me, but I kept going. I didn't complain, I just did what I had to do.

The 2nd Time Around

My mother in law eventually came, and such a burden was lifted. She helped me in so many ways she would never know! Well Grandma Doria Hampton, if I haven't told you enough THANK YOU! Let me talk about Grandma for a moment. I had the BEST in LAWS a girl could ask for! All love, and NO DRAMA! The family survived off LOVE, and it was very attractive! My father in law had passed the year we moved to Texas, but that man was so generous and full of laughs. When I tell you, his smile was CONTAGIOUS! I mean just that. It was beautiful, just as he was. My in laws always handled me with care. I was just blessed to have them. I had one request that I didn't share, when Grandpa passed away, I asked God if he would please allow me to see him again. He was a dad, a protector, and dared anyone to mess with me! I have this one story I remember, one day the kids and I went to visit them and I was parking the car. They lived in Los Angeles County and the street was kind of narrow. He's smiling and waiting for me to park, because I was pregnant with Latte (Auriana) at the time. But out of nowhere, this car came speeding down the street, and nicked my mirror on the driver side! I was shocked and a bit shaken up, but when I looked up, Grandpa, just that quick had a bat in his hand and was as ready to go after whoever it was! He called me JA-LINDA, because he really couldn't pronounce my name, it was so funny. He was like "Jalinda, you alright fatso?" HAAAA because I was pregnant with the big belly! He said, "Because I was going to knock him out!" Such great memories. RIP Willie G. Hampton. To this day, I don't know how Grandpa got that bat so fast! When he passed, God did

Becoming the Widow

grant my request. I saw Grandpa in a dream. He was so happy and he had made it to HEAVEN!

Now for my mother in law, she's a quiet giant! She offered to come help me. I would say by now it was time because things were getting hectic. Grandma went to the hospital every single day! She stayed there and watched her son. What a mother's love! She would come to the house for a few hours and would be ready to go back. She never left her son's side. Meanwhile, it was getting a bit overbearing, so I continued to thank God for HIS covering and having someone as special as herself to help me in ways she probably to this day doesn't know. I did everything the best I could and handled everything the best way I knew how, but I felt like I was crumbling. My husband started telling me secrets, things that I didn't want to address, and he would tell me I wasn't listening. That's how I knew he was serious. Hampton was 12 years older than me and he had so much wisdom. He was an excellent teacher! I believe it to be true, he was by far a genius! I'm not just saying that, but he was so Anointed. His demeanor was so powerful, yet he was 'Gawdsrvnt' (God's Servant) He spelled it that way and I thought it was kind of cool. When I would spend the night in the hospital with him, every time the buzzer would go off, my husband would jump! From such a strong man, in his frailty, but he was more so concerned about others. The announcement would say, CODE BLUE, CODE BLUE! You would hear the shuffling, the fast movements outside the door, the nurses going back and forth, and all this commotion. Hampton would squeeze my hand and whisper, "Lord, I hope it wasn't one of my friends." Everyone on that level had some form of cancer, and once the buzzer went off, he would squeeze my hand, and say "Babe, lets pray for the families." We didn't know who they were, but just the fact of hearing "CODE BLUE", we knew someone's family member would get the bad news shortly. On one night, it was CODE BLUE three times that night, and my husband would keep his eyes closed, and immediately go into prayer. To watch this man, and to see how big his heart was, I was in awe and amazement!

Grandma was with us for over a month, and she was heading back home. She told me if I needed ANYTHING to let her know. Well, she's always been that way with me. She's still that way with me to this day!

As a daughter in law, we have had our talks, some more uncomfortable than others, but she's out right amazing! She's so small in stature but gentle in her spirit. Sometimes I don't even think she knows how much of a blessing she is to myself, as well as my babies! Grandma Doria Hampton, I just LOVE HER!

The chemo was taking a toll on my husband, and one day he told me they were giving him 33 hours of chemo straight! Well, we won't go into how I really feel about that. Like seriously, who can handle all of that? I let Grandma know and she asked me if I wanted her to come back. I told her no, that we were hopeful, and Hampton was getting out of the hospital soon. The last time my husband was admitted in the hospital to stay, it was on our youngest daughter's birthday, Auriana (Latte, as we call her). He didn't get out of the hospital until the last Friday of the month. I waited to celebrate my girl's birthday, because clearly, they wanted daddy to be home!! We were soooooo happy that Hampton was able to come home. My husband was so frail and weak. He had lost all is hair, eyebrows, and he was 164lbs. My strong man, what happened? I had to handle him with care. His every move, I was right there, asking what can I do? I was so determined to get him back to health. I remember I had a specific product and asked him if he wanted some. He literally drank two cups and kept it down. I believe in my heart that the product was a miracle for my husband, because that big tumor mass he had on his neck was gone in two days. YES, a MIRACLE! Also, he was able to drink the product without vomiting, which meant a lot to me. That tumor had gotten so big that it pushed my husband's head to the side. Tilt your head as far as you can to the right! Although he was looking straight at you, his head was tilted because the tumor had gotten so big! Well, I tell you what! THAT DEVIL IS A LIE! After drinking the product, the tumor was gone. His head and neck were back to normal, but he had lymphoma in his neck and chest. Prior to all this, my husband had his yearly physical in July and everything came back normal. It appeared that he had a clean bill of health. How did we go from a good report, to two small knots that grew into a big mass, to chemo, in less than two months?

The 2nd Time Around

The day of my girls' party, my husband was too weak to go. But when we came home, we loved on him for the remainder of the evening. It was so much LOVE in the midst, so many smiles, hugs, and gentle kisses. I knew Hampton was getting better!

Things just felt normal with him home. I paid attention. I didn't let Hampton out of my sight. I started taking off work, just so that I could be with him. It was so much better than having to drive all the way to Dallas and back, 51 miles one-way. Wheeewwwww, that was crazy and past exhausting.

On February 1st, 2010 and believe me I wouldn't have even noticed this date, but it was a Monday, and we have choir rehearsal on Mondays. I made sure Hampton was okay. He told me to go to rehearsal and leave the kids with him. I did! When I got back home, he was resting and he had his eyes closed. I did my normal check in, gave him a kiss, and asked how he was doing. He said he was okay and I told him I was going to take a shower. When I got out the shower, I thought he was sleep. I started to get in the bed and he said, "Babe, the Lord said to anoint my head." One thing I know about my husband is if he said it, then it was accurate. He had just that type of relationship with the Lord. I can't even begin to express how Anointed this man was. I didn't understand why, but I began to pray, while touching his head. "AMEN!" I said when I was done. He replied "AMEN!" I went into the bathroom again for something and he called me again. I came to the door quickly. He said, "The Lord said to do it again!" Okay now, sheesh! Was I not anointed enough? Did I not do it right? All sorts of things went through my head. Is my heart, right? I did a self-check quickly, and of course, now I have butterflies of nervousness, because I'm not quite sure where this is going! I prayed again. Afterwards, he said, "That's it. Thank you." and he went to sleep. I was mostly confused, but I felt better knowing that he felt satisfied with the request and plea I had made to God on his behalf.

It was approximately 2:30 a.m., and I heard, BOOOOOOOM, BAMMMMMM, BOOOOOOMMMMM. I jumped up! Frantic, I knew something was wrong, my heart was beating so fast, my house was pitch black, and all lights were out. I felt for Hampton, and he wasn't in the bed! I jumped up, running carefully throughout the house, because I didn't know where he was. I don't know why, but it was almost like I couldn't find the lights or anything! No Hampton in the room, the hallway, but when I got into the kitchen, there he was shaking on the floor. It was like a horror film. I couldn't even scream, JESUS! I thought. What happened? My husband was shaking, his eyes were rolling behind his head, and the blood started coming out of his head. I SWEAR to you I thought I was in a nightmare! I WISH I could say that's what is was, but it was real life! OHHH my GOD! I'm crying, I'm frantic, I run to get my cell phone, and of course I can't find it. JESUS! I ran back into the kitchen. My cell phone was in my purse! I dial 911. I could barely talk. I was shaking. Blood had covered at least a third of the floor and it could have been more. It was like a movie when someone gets shot, and the blood just start pouring

The 2nd Time Around

out. The lady was very calm, and she was telling me that I couldn't touch him because we didn't know if his neck was broke or not! HUH? How does she even know to tell me all of this? By this time, Hampton came to himself. He was like, "Babe, why won't you help me up?" I lost it. I started crying so bad. He kept asking me to help him and I just grabbed his hand. I said, "Hampton, the lady told me not to move you. Someone is coming to help you!" He said, "Babe, please help me, its cold down here!" The tears are flowing as we speak. Have you ever been in a situation where there was NOTHING you could do at that moment? Well, that was me! I felt so helpless. I wanted him to get off the floor so bad, and truthfully, he didn't even know who I was when he initially woke up! By now, the ambulance has come into the house, I'm crying uncontrollably. I'm in a panic, although I did listen to the 911 operator, I had her on speaker, and she kept saying, "Ma'am, I know this is hard, but you don't want to hurt your husband, so please don't move him." I was screaming on the inside, literally! I called my pastor or someone, I can't remember it was two in the morning, and I told them I had to go to the hospital. It seems like everything I did that night was pointing toward me! Why didn't I feel Hampton get up? Just this one time. I didn't feel him. Hampton never wanted me to see him in that state, so when he would be in the bathroom vomiting, if I would enter that bathroom, he would tell me to get out. He never wanted me to see him suffering! But this one time, I didn't feel him get out of bed. Hampton was trying to get him some water, slipped in his vomit, hit his head on the kitchen counter, the kitchen island, and then the tile floor. He busted his head wide open, literally!

We are now in trauma, room four, and his head looks so bad, and he kept apologizing to me! I was like, "Babe, it's not your fault and I'm so sorry I didn't hear you get up." He was hoping to be quiet and not wake me up, but that noise was so bad, I woke up crying! He was calm. I made the calls to his mom and my pastor, and they asked to please keep them informed.

Things seemed stable, but Hampton kept apologizing. He also said, "I'm sorry I made you miss work today." I'm like, "Babe, don't worry. When they fix your head, we are going to go home and cuddle!" I really thought that's what we were going to do. I never imagined in a million years that would be my last day with him! JESUS!

He started talking to me and telling me more things, the secrets as I call them. Hampton told me specifics. He said, "Babe, your knight in shining armor is going to come get you. He's going to love you and my babies as if they are his own..." I started shaking my head in disbelief, and I'm like, "NOOO Hampton! What are you talking about? You are my knight in shining armor!" He said, "Babe, you are not listening." Well, remember I told you when he would say that, I knew he was serious! "Your knight in shining armor is going to come get you. He is going to love you and the kids so much, you will RE-MARRY, and he will take care of you!" I cried like a baby! Why is he saying this stuff? Maybe he's a little confused from the fall, but I knew better, he was very comprehensive! He also said, "OHHHH and that situation," He pointed at my BREAST! He said, "Your testimony is going to WOW the world!" I get goose bumps every time I repeat that, and every time, I think of that moment. At that time, I didn't even know what the SITUATION WAS! WOW, Hampton...so accurate...so anointed. Let me paint the picture for you from that very day! You are reading this book! What a testimony. My testimony will WOW the WORLD! #tearsofJOY! Thank you, Hampton, Thank you!

The nurse came in and she had a big needle. She told me it was going to be at least 70-75 stitches to patch Hampton back together. She proceeded to give Hampton a shot with that big needle at least the length of a pencil, if not longer, but when she put the needle in his head, he didn't budge! She stuck him again, and if I'm not mistaken, it was three times. He never flinched! "Hampton, that doesn't hurt you?" I asked. He grabbed his head, literally, you can see the blood, and the meat. I'm telling you, it was so graphic. Yes, his head was split open. He grabbed his head, and said, "NO, it's okay, it doesn't hurt." Now I know goodness well, he had to be in pain. There's no way, even from the fall, his head had to be hurting! I started praying amongst myself, "Lord, is this why you had me anoint his head? Did he not feel any of this?" Hampton was thirsty. He kept asking for juice. I was trying to find someone to help me, but it was so much going on, the nurse would say, "Okay, I will bring it." Then he would ask me again for juice, and he kept telling me stuff I had no clue about. For instance, he said

Becoming the Widow

"Babe, I want you to know that I asked the Lord to take me home." What? He said, "I asked the Lord to take me home!" Immediately, I thought how selfish is this? How do you just opt out and leave me here with these kids, by myself? "No, now see you are really talking crazy!" I told him. He said, "Babe, you're not listening." This is way too much, I thought! "Babe, listen to me," I said, "We are about to go home, we are going to get some rest, and everything will be fine!" He replied, "Babe, you are not listening." He now has his juice. He told me everything all over again; I would re-marry, I would be happy, and he already made sure we would be well taking care of. At this point I'm listening, but I'm so confused. The staff is about to sow his head back together, and we were going home! He started talking about God and how his only other concern was that he made it in to Heaven. He started talking about how glorious this place called Heaven is, and that he knew we were going to be fine. He blessed me so much, because think about this: for a man, who I know for a fact loved his family, to bless us to have a joyous life, with someone else! No, that's not selfish, its SELFLESS!

In that moment, I'm not quite sure what Hampton saw, but it was something. He was so intrigued by it, it was like he was staring off, but the smile on his face, and then... BEEEEEEEPPPPPPP, everything flat lined, he stopped breathing! "Somebody please help me!" I yelled as loud as I could. People came running from everywhere! All sorts of chaos, RUNNING IN AND OUT OF THE ROOM! They worked on Hampton, and worked on Hampton, and I remember counting eleven people in

The 2nd Time Around

the room. The doctor was on top of him, pressing his chest constantly, and I was like, "Man, not so hard," but these were all the thoughts going through my head and I couldn't even think straight! They pushed and yelled, "Hampton, wake up!" They talked and talked, and then finally he came back to life! WHEEEEWWWWWW. See, like I said, we are going home after all of this. I stood there holding his hand, and HE TOLD me HE LOVED me, and again, whatever he saw, the look was like he was saying he was sorry. But whatever he was seeing, he wanted that more! Moments later, it happened again. All these doctors were everywhere! And they kept working on him, switching off, then someone else would try, and nothing! They closed the curtain! And literally, my LIFE, every memory, every moment, our whole entire marriage flashed right before my eyes! Lord, please, NO! Please! Please, don't let it be! Lord, please! Whatever I've done, please Lord, don't. The doctor came from behind the curtain. And he said, "Mrs. Hampton, I'm so sorry. Your husband has passed away!" "No, No, No, No No NO!" I said it over and over! This pain is like nothing I've ever felt in my life! I remember grabbing him. "What am I supposed do?" I YELLED! "What am I supposed to tell my kids?" It wasn't a yell, I could barely get the questions out. He said, "I'm so sorry!" Man, talking about feeling like you are in a horror movie! My mind was racing 1000 miles per second. What in the world was I going to do? "Noooooo, go do something, fix it please!" I literally fell to the ground, balled up in the corner, and wept! When you lose a loved one, especially someone you adore, someone you admire, someone you are extremely close with, to hear those words, "I'm sorry, we've done all we could," YOUR LIFE literally stops! It is so PAINFUL and GUT WRENCHING. Like getting hit by a MACK TRUCK while someone is stabbing you in the same places a thousand times over, and you know what? As much as I'm trying to get you to understand the hurt, I know this explanation is not doing any JUSTICE for what I felt in that moment. Hampton was gone. My husband, my friend! GONE! February 2nd, 2010, my husband was GONE!

Everything was a blur! I couldn't think, sleep, nor eat. I remember calling my mother in law. That was the worst phone call I've ever had to make in my life! I called my mom, she was working for MTA at the time, and she said, "Shalana, I'm so sorry. Let me turn this bus around, I will see you later!" I really didn't catch what she said or what she really meant! The call to my pastor, cut me real deep. Hampton was a servant leader, he was an Elder in whom my pastor could trust. I knew he would be heart broken. I hated to make those calls, and to this day, those who know me, know I do NOT LIKE THE PHONES! I sat in that room and I cried for what seemed to be hours. I cried in disbelief. Maybe he would wake up, and I was thinking take that sheet off him just in case he woke up! My pastor came to the hospital, and all I heard was, "Sis. Hampton, I'm so sorry." I cried and cried. I just can't believe this! I even asked my pastor, "What am I supposed to do? What am I supposed to tell my babies?" It appeared that no one had answers for me! The chaplain came. We talked, well,

The 2nd Time Around

they talked to me. I was zoned out. We prayed, but why weren't my prayers working? Well, I will tell you why. Listen to me closely...I don't care what the situation is, God is able! However, if a person's prayer is different than yours, you can pray until you are blue in the face. I knew my husband had a relationship with the Lord, and I recall, he said, "Babe, I asked the Lord to take me home." He said that he lived his life. Really? He was only 45! And he told me I had a WHOLE LIFE ahead OF ME! So, if the prayers are not on one accord, then, well, let's just say it's not that your prayers aren't being answered, it just may not be God's will. And clearly, I was not going to say, "Not my will, Lord, but YOURS!" Oh no, I didn't want those results. So, I was praying for my husband to live. Meanwhile, Hampton was tired! Always remember God knows BEST, and HE can do ANYTHING BUT FAIL!

Becoming the Widow

REFLECTING MOMENTS

Has there been a time when perhaps you've lost a loved one, where you had to ingest that God knows what's best? And you knew not YOUR WILL, but the WILL OF THE LORD? Reflect on this, or these times, and acknowledge how God gave you comfort.

_____
_____
_____
_____
_____
_____
_____
_____
_____
_____
_____
_____
_____
_____
_____
_____
_____
_____
_____
_____

The 2nd Time Around

Chapter 6

Torture and Nightmares

My kids were asleep. They each had their own room, Tyion, Amiyah, and Auriana. All their bedrooms were upstairs, while mine was downstairs. All the lights were out, and I had my typical routine in which I did the same thing every night. Once I knew they were fast asleep, I would make my rounds around the house. I would walk all throughout the house, go into each of their rooms, and make sure everything was secure. Doors locked, garage door leading into the house was locked, back door locked, I checked everything. This night, I was watching a little TV until I got sleepy. I remembered I turned the TV off, got comfortable and closed my eyes. Lights out...

The house was so quiet you could hear a pin drop! It was taking some time for me to FALL ASLEEP! I looked to the ceiling, and just stared at how dark the room was. I switched positions, thinking it would help, and I couldn't seem to get comfortable. I turned back over to the left

The 2nd Time Around

side and stretched a bit more! Part of my left hand was under my head, and now my eyes were closed. For some reason, I felt cold. It was like a rush of cold air came into the room. I remember shaking and shivering. I pulled the covers up even higher and proceeded to warm up. I tucked my feet into the covers, and I had the comforter touching my face. By now I'm lying on my back, and I was thinking. Now I'm tired, but I can't go to sleep. Then it happened again, a rush of cold air breezed its way into my room. I'm not afraid of the dark, so I just laid there. I knew my air conditioner wasn't on, so why was I feeling super cold? Eyes closed and FINALLY trying to get to sleep! Out of nowhere, I was being held down! Scooching from side to side, trying to move! I couldn't MOVE! I COULDN'T SEE, because it was so dark... but something was holding me! WHAT IS THIS? I THOUGHT OF MY BABIES. My instincts were to get up and get to them, but I COULDN'T MOVE! Tears started rolling down my face and I SCREAMED and YELLED as loud as I could only to find out my mouth was covered. Wait a minute, I can't move, I can't scream... what is this? I yelled again and NOTHING came out. I tried to move as much as I could, and I wasn't getting anywhere! My tears are flowing; I'm shaking my head as fast as I can from side to side, but when I did that something grabbed my forehead... I started to move my arms, but I could only move my fingers! JESUS! Where are my babies? NO ONE COULD HEAR ME! Whatever, WHOEVER this is, I can barely breathe! My mouth was covered along with part of my nose, with just enough room to get small breaths in... I was panicking and I was breathing so fast. My heart was

Torture and Nightmares

racing, and I thought of a time when this lady at a visiting church was giving her testimony, and she was in a situation where she couldn't even talk. She was in the hospital bed and she mentioned that it's a HORRIBLE feeling to wake up and not be able to move. I remembered her testimony so vividly, and she said, "All I could do was yell JESUS in MY MIND!" JESUS! JESUS! JESUS! What a gut-wrenching feeling, when you are held and bound against your will. When you can't even defend yourself or move for that matter! My mind was racing a million miles per second and I just wanted to make sure my babies were ok! I was thinking whatever this is, it must know I would have fought back, that's why so many of them were holding me down! Gosh, what punks I thought, to where you can't even take me one on one. As sure as my name is what it is, I promise you, if I would have been able to have some motion, I would have knocked this thing out into the middle of next week! I mean that with all my heart! How dare you jump me like this, and you don't even fight fair! What LOSERS, I thought! I couldn't even budge! I yelled, "JESUS", in my head as many times as I needed to, until whatever it was had left me alone. I jumped up and ran upstairs, praying on the way up there. "Lord, please, my babies, Lord please, my babies, don't let anything have happened to them... Lord please!" First room, checked, Amiyah was sound to sleep, then Tyion, check, sound to sleep, I was pulling covers back to make sure I didn't see anything. I checked closets and checked their bathroom. Third room, check, Auriana, fast to sleep. My heart was literally jumping out of my chest. I sat on the top step and I just cried. For more than one reason. I was so happy that my babies weren't harmed first. Then secondly, I was so thankful that whoever it was didn't kill me! But wait a minute... Who was it? I thought. Everything is locked. There's no sign of breaking in and I never heard voices, so what was that? I cried until I felt safe to walk back down stairs to get back into bed. My prayer went extremely long that night, but who could I tell? No one would believe me... not with that type of story. I tried to block it out and I convinced myself that I had a nightmare. HMMMPFFFF some NIGHTMARE!

The so called "nightmares" got worse and worse! For the sake of KNOWING, when whoever or WHATEVER would come, the coldness and the sounds would get louder and louder! Before it would hold me down and torture me, and I mean that literally, I would start crying out to God! One time, I was able to get some sound out, and it seemed like that thing was super MAD! It wrestled with me for what seemed to be HOURS! It was early morning by the time IT decided to leave me alone.

The torture, nightmares, and torment continued. I was so mentally exhausted! I didn't know who I could talk to, but I knew I needed some help! Obviously by now I mean I guess it's safe to say, there were no physical people in my house when I endured the torture! I prayed over myself daily, and I knew that I had to continuously pray for my mind! Pray, that I wouldn't completely lose it. I've seen it happen before, not to me of course, but to someone I know. If you don't have your mind, well really you aren't working with much! Have you ever heard the term, "the

Torture and Nightmares

mind is a terrible thing to waste?" It's so true and in this sense, if you lose your mind, then you are completely out of control with self! Well, what I had left, I held on to it. I knew better. I knew God could turn this thing around, I didn't understand why suddenly, and why I would be a target again, but Lord, please just don't let me lose my mind.

I remember when I was 17, for the first time I saw someone for what they were dealing with. It wasn't a pretty sight. Whatever this thing was, it was ugly. I saw it in the spirit, and the Lord would typically show me things that I didn't want to know. I prayed over and over, to take it away. I didn't want to see these things for what they were. Lord, please, take this away, and for years, I didn't activate it. I didn't use the gift. I didn't want to, I wanted NO PARTS of it! I just didn't want to deal with it. Anyway, as I got older, and when I realized I was being tormented and attacked, I knew what I was REALLY dealing with. I had a conversation with one of my girlfriends, and it just so happened she was talking about deliverance and how she needed God to help her through some things that she was experiencing. I was so RELIEVED that finally now I can confide into someone and let her know what I was experiencing, and maybe, just maybe she could help me. Well, I didn't bring it up the first time, but as we got closer in our sisterhood, I felt more comfortable to share. She was a little older than me in age, and her testimony was amazing. When I expressed what I had been experiencing, she immediately told me that I needed deliverance. She had a place for me to go, and I also attended a service, where I was able to experience the deliverance service. I felt so relieved. I felt so good, I felt much better. Although mentally exhausted, I understood what I experienced. I also read a book called, *When the Pigs Move In*, by Don Dickerman. Man, when I tell you, I learned so much about deliverance and that ministry. This situation was real and I didn't have time to play with it. I HAD TO FIGHT! I studied, I engaged, and I was willing to face this situation with all my might! I was ready for battle, and as clear as I saw the last night I was supposed to be tortured, I called that thang out, and I told it, not tonight! For whatever reason, now that I think about it, any other time I wouldn't be able to talk, but this time, I was bold, and I said, "YOUR TIME IS UP, YOU HAVE TO GO in JESUS' name!" I saw such an ugly whatever you would want to call it, gray skin, and wrinkled, hunched over, looking back at me, with those big hideous eyes, and I said it again, "Your time is up! You must GO! In JESUS NAME!" And whatever it was, it disappeared!

My deliverance had been received. I learned so much in this duration. I really started understanding the POWER of the TONGUE! And although that assignment was assigned to wiped me out, IT WAS CANCELLED!

I can't honestly say that it never happened again, but what I can say is, that it was more afraid of me. Spiritually I was refueled, and every time I would get a visit, I could tell it was getting weaker and weaker!

Chapter 7

God Equipping You for the TASK!

The bible says, God will never put more on you than you can bear. You can't get any more accurate than this. I truly believe everything that God has ALLOWED to happen, it was for a reason. Whether it's to strengthen you in some areas where you are weak, or to increase your level of faith, or it could just be simply a test so that you can endure something for someone else! I ALSO FEEL THAT WE GO THROUGH THINGS FOR OTHER PEOPLE. For instance: I couldn't tell you how many people who have crossed my path since my testimony, who have come to me, called, texted, Facebook messaged me, emailed me, just to get encouragement because now they are going through the same thing or they know someone with a similar experience. Now clearly the bible says we overcome by the words of our testimonies. And although some things seem more drastic than others, trust me, if you are going through it, YOU CAN HANDLE IT!

Many people go through things and handle certain experiences differently. So, it's crucial to be VERY careful with how you speak to people, how you treat people, and truly what you think of people! People are people just like you, but think about it, you never know what a person is going through. Now seriously, do I look like I had breast cancer? Do I look like I'm a widow? And I'm sure these things that I'm sharing is pretty Shocking! That's where the saying goes, YOU NEVER KNOW WHAT A PERSON IS GOING THROUGH! Those are my thoughts exactly. You know the term "You can't judge a book by its cover?" Well, that's EXACTLY what I MEAN, because you just simply may never know!

There were so many different aspects that I used for SURVIVAL! Another one of my main sources is a book called *Prayers that Move Mountains* by John Eckhardt. The whole entire source helps activate and allow you to demolish any mountain you may be facing. As I mentioned before, words are POWERFUL, so the scripture says: "For verily I say unto you, that whosoever shall say unto this mountain, be thou removed, and be cast into the sea; and shall not doubt in his heart but shall believe that those things which he saith shall come to pass; he shall have whatsoever he saith." Mark 11 :23 NKJ.

One of the prayers that I specifically targeted in the book was the chapter on prayer and fasting. The reason why is

God Equipping You for the TASK!

because when you are dealing with situations that seem impossible to come out of, there are just some things that will ONLY BREAK THROUGH FASTING AND PRAYING! "And he said unto them, this kind can come forth by NOTHING, but by prayer and fasting." Mark 9:29. In other words, there are certain situations and certain circumstances that it doesn't matter what you do, your situation will not change UNLESS you pray and FAST!

Specifically, there was one prayer out of the book which read: "Fasting breaks the mountain of sickness and infirmity and releases healing. (Isaiah 58:5-6,8) Fasting can help eliminate chronic sicknesses and diseases. Lastly, God has PROMISED that our health will spring forth speedily.

Side note: your fasting MUST BE genuine, not religious or hypocritical! (John Eckhardt) I like to use the analogy of organic produce or anything that is organic for that matter. It's pure, and not saturated with GMO's. It doesn't contain harmful chemicals that will jeopardize its authenticity. Organic and PURE is how your prayer and fasting should be.

Chapter 8

The 2nd Time Around

You are not going to believe this! After being equipped for the task, for every new level, it's a new devil. Have you ever heard that? It might sound cliché-ish, but that's what I was feeling. Going back to "The rush back to Texas," I wasn't fully settled. However, I decided to go to California to visit for the summer. I remember before I left, I was upstairs praying in the play room, and I remember the Lord spoke to me. LIVE! See, it's sooooo important not to be distracted. And although I was facing something, I had every reason valid enough to be completely distracted. However, I heard it so clear. So, I confirmed the flights for my three children as well as myself, and we were off to Cali as soon as school let out for that summer! It had been quite some time since we had visited, so we were all excited and ready to go.

Upon arrival, I had sooo many fun things planned for my girls. It was a good welcome home visit, and my mom thought she was kind of slick. When it would get close to our time to leave, she would suggest extending my stay. And of course, we were having such a great time, I extended my stay three times!

When I express "The 2nd Time Around," I mean in terms of this condition. Remember the doctors in Virginia that didn't want to move forward with surgery for six months? But as I continued to seek the Lord, HE TOLD ME SPECIFICALLY TO LIVE!

Another one of my favorite scriptures that speaks to the depth of my soul always is: II Chronicles 7:14

"If my people who are called by my name, would humble themselves and pray, and seek my face, and turn from their wicked ways; then will I hear from Heaven, and forgive their sin, and will Heal their land."

What a Powerful set of words!

I remember I was in prayer and I asked God, "What was the cure for breast cancer?" I said "Lord, if you just give me the formula, I promise I will share it. There are so many women who get hit with this terrible dis-ease because their bodies are UN-eased. Many of them have experienced traumatic challenges, and life itself can seem so unfair!" I prayed and I kept asking, because I really wanted to know. There are visions and things that GOD has promised me, but this breast cancer stuff we MUST NIP this in the bud! I bind and rebuke any attack over my family life! Generational curses? Yep, those exist. I only

The 2nd Time Around

believe it will continue if you DO NOT SEVER it at the ROOT!

Listen to me, my grandmother, bless her heart, was the best. Let me explain how beautiful this jewel was; she was chocolate, with ocean blue eyes and silver hair...She was such a beauty! Matter of fact, she was GORGEOUS! I watched her growing up. I watched her life, and she was amazing! She loved the Lord and had a voice like a song bird. Although I knew at times when she would sing she had more on the inside, she seemed shy. She was such a giver and would give the clothes off her back! We were ALWAYS blessing others, from singing in nursing homes, to getting household supplies and food for various families. She was so BLESSED, because she ALWAYS BLESSED OTHERS! But I guess it was because of age, and outside the fact that I lived a lot of my childhood in another country (West Germany). But when I was around her, that's all I remember. As I grew older, I found out that her older sister had passed away from breast cancer, and then one of her living sisters now, had breast cancer! Then there's me! But you know what? THE DEVIL IS A LIE! And I will SEVER this attack at the root and send the attack back to the pit of hell so that it SHALL NEVER RETURN! This is my prayer, this is my plea. I know for a fact my granny went through these things for me, and I also know that I have gone through the same things for the sake of others. As far as my children and my children's children, I demand, and declare, and decree in the name of JESUS that NONE OF THEM will experience what I have! IT STOPS NOW! And I mean RIGHT NOW!

The 2nd Time Around

Father God we thank you for your blood that will NEVER LOSE ITS POWER! THE BLOOD of the savior, IT STILL WORKS! The song writer said, "It reaches to the highest mountains, and it FLOWS to the lowest valley, the blood that gives me strength from day to day, it WILL NEVER LOSE ITS POWER!" That's old school in case you didn't know! But the words are so powerful, no matter how well you are doing in life, or how low you *may fall, the Blood of God can wash you, cleanse you, and make you over again! I can't help it, it's just in me, the word of GOD WILL KEEP YOU!*

Now back to my prayer. Lord what is the cure? And it was like I was in a movie! I saw the BIGGEST LETTER 'I', the BIGGEST LETTER 'A', and the BIGGEST LETTER 'M', as HIGH as I could see in the clouds! Then I heard a response:

I AM! My God in Heaven! I will never forget that day, so I took my testimony and I ran with it.

The bible says, "He was wounded for our transgressions, and bruised for our inequities: the chastisement of our peace was upon him and with his stipes we are healed!" Isaiah 53:5. So in other words, HE already went through IT for YOU! When the Lord showed me those three letters, I AM, I was in such awwwwwwawwe! Sometimes we make things so complicated to where we miss the message! God said HE was the CURE, bottom line! AHHH so in effort for your healing, you must go through HIM first. Well, at least that's what I BELIEVE!

The 2nd Time Around

Chapter 9

The First Angel Visit

When the Holy Spirit Speaks, be prepared to move in action. That was something that I heard constantly upon my return to Texas. I was so happy to have made that decision to go back, and my natural treatments were in full effect. I wanted to get better so badly that I attended the facility at least four times a week. It was so important to me at any cost to BE WELL! But my experience there was so angelic! One day, I was getting ozone therapy treatment in my ears. That's where you are given increased oxygen supply, because when the body is at an alkaline state, DISEASE can't live there! The ozone ear therapy was used to treat imbalances in the body ranging from viral infections to cancer (source: House of Gilead).

To the natural eye, I was in bad shape. The tumor was getting bigger, and as the doctor prayed for me, I knew we were on a mission to have a victorious outcome! So, this day I was getting the ozone ear therapy and there was a lady there, who was so cute! She was an older lady, and she was receiving ozone therapy on her hands! I didn't know at the time why she would need the treatment on her hands, but we both smiled and spoke to each other. She asked me my name, and she told me her name was Priscilla. "So nice to meet you, Ms. Priscilla," I replied. We were having general conversation, and of course we got on the subject as to why I was there. I gave her a brief summary about the loss of my husband and having a double mastectomy three months after my husband passed. She indicated how strong I was to have endured such tragedies. However, she encouraged me. I really liked her. Her personality was so calming. The staff came to get me to take me into a different room, and she said, "See you next time!" I proceeded to follow the young lady who was taking me into another room and I started my next treatment, the RIFE Therapy. Dr. RIFE used a plasma tube device. The RIFE machine actually works at a cellular level in effort to do one or two things: 1. kill Pathogens, or 2. support the body's system. This is a non-invasive procedure allowing the scanned frequencies to target viruses, bacteria, parasites, and other disease models (Article, RIFETech). I love natural treatment, because there are so many ways you could connect the body for healing.

While I was enjoying the treatment, I heard a woman down the hall. Her voice was very shaky and fragile. As the voice got a bit closer, I could tell the lady was crying. I couldn't hear what she was saying, but I could tell she was emotional. I was new to this facility, so I didn't know

The First Angel Visit

of anyone in there, so I just closed my eyes, and continued with my RIFE TREAMENT. The voice got closer, so close, I could hear two people talking right outside my door. "NO!" The woman said, her voice was shivering, she said "She was just here." The staff was very patient with her, and replied "Ma'am, I'm not sure who you are talking about." By this time the lady was crying so heavily she could barely get the words out. I couldn't see them, I could only hear the two of them talking. "She was so beautiful! I talked to her, I HAVE TO TELL HER SOMETHING." the woman who was crying said. "Ma'am, please don't get yourself all upset. We will try to help you. But honestly, I didn't see anyone like you are describing!" She said, "I forgot her name, but she was tall. She had brown skin and long hair!" Wait a minute! I thought to myself. Tall, well I'm 5'8", I do have brown skin except my legs, because those need a tan, and really long hair, well I definitely have that! GOODNESS! It was like the light bulb went off. Could she be talking… noooooo, couldn't be… wait a minute, is this lady talking about me? The one thing I appreciate, whomever this lady was speaking of, the staff was determined to find them for her. She kept describing as the staff was trying to console her. I could hear the lady crying frantically. I was wondering, what happened? And if she was talking about me, what did she need to tell me?

One more step, and the woman was in my doorway! It was Ms. Priscilla! The sweet lady I had met earlier! When we made eye contact, she said "There she is!" as she was walking towards me. She said crying frantically, "I have to tell you something! God told me to tell you something," she said. She didn't care who was around, nor who was watching. By this time, I was ready to receive whatever it was she had to say. I could tell she was sincere; you couldn't fake that type of cry! "Psalms, 118," she said while taking in heavy deep breaths, "READ THE WHOLE CHAPTER! You will LIVE to DECLARE HIS WORKS! When you get to verse 18, then you will know what I'm talking about." WOWWWWWWWWW! What a Blessing! I felt the presence of GOD. I felt that HE was there with me and giving me comfort. From a natural point of view, my health was in trouble, but God sent a CONFIRMING WORD! I WILL LIVE! I gave her a hug and thanked her for the word. I closed my eyes, and immediately went into PRAISE! God is so merciful! He is so merciful! Wow, what a wonderful experience! I knew I was at the right place, at the right time! My God, what a Mighty GOD WE SERVE!

My daily routine was so structured and I loved my treatment days. It put me into an element of happiness!!! I met so many wonderful people from all over the globe! I saw miracles happen with my own two eyes. People were being RESTORED, REVIVED, and RENEWED! People were LIVING AGAIN! God was in the midst! It was an experience that I will never forget. During my different treatment settings, I would just converse with God, and praise my way to a LEVEL of belief that is second to none. I was no better than anyone else, yet I was humbled to know God chose me for this task.

The First Angel Visit

Time had passed, weeks to be exact! I was feeling so good on the inside! MY hopes were high, and my faith was untouched!

The room was quiet, other than the Christian music playing in the background. At the time, I didn't know the name of this singing group, but I had learned the words of the song!

HA-LE-LUJAH- You have WON the Victory!!!! Hallelujah you have WON it ALL for ME!!!! Death could not HOLD you down, you are the risen King, Seated in Majesty, you are the RISEN KING!!!!!!! ~ Planet Shakers

Once the song came on, I got super excited, and I was lying on the BIOMAT. It felt so good on my body and the heat, the crystals, all that! I was so comfortable, but I was kind of sleepy! I was singing the words to myself with my eyes closed, tears beginning to flow, yet I kept my eyes closed. That environment was so soothing! Then suddenly, I heard, "Shalana! Psssst! Shalana!" while touching my feet! I woke up, and it was a lady at the foot of my bed! She was rubbing my feet! She said, "Everything is going to be okay!" She was so beautiful and had the most gorgeous smile! I looked, trying to zoom in, because my eyes had tears in them! She said, "YOU'RE GOING TO LIVE!" I don't remember seeing this lady, since I had been receiving treatments. But she was amazingly gorgeous! She said, "Shalana, YOU ARE GOING TO LIVE!" When she said it the last time, the RIFE bar was in my hand, and it touched my face! When

The 2nd Time Around

that happened, I WOKE UP! I WAS ASLEEP! I started looking around the room. Where did that lady go? I know what I saw. I got up! I sat on the bio mat, and I was just thinking. I looked in the hallway, and there was no sign of her. I laid back down on the bio mat, my heart was racing quite a bit, because the experience was so real. The timer went off, and one of the staff came into the room to attend to me. She said "How do you feel? I said "Good, I took a nap! And the bio-mat was soooo warm!" She said, "GOOOD! I'm glad you enjoyed it." Then I said, "Excuse me, ma'am, what's the lady name with the long white and silver hair?" She said "Excuse me?" "There was a lady in my room. She had long, white and silver hair." She said, "When was she in your room?" "Just now!" I replied. "She literally was just standing here!" The young lady looked at me a bit confused, and then she said, "Well, did she have on scrubs like me? What color were they?" I said, "No, she had on a long white robe!" She said, "Really?" As her face perked up. But I was so serious, because I needed to tell her THANK YOU! She said, "A long white robe, huh?" "Yes," I replied eager to get her name. She said "Honey, THAT WAS YOUR ANGEL! There's no woman here with that on!" And I thought about it! I thought I was awake when the lady touched my feet, but, I was asleep! I felt a warm sense of comfort hovering over me, and once again, I started rejoicing and thanking God for yet again sending me comfort!

The lady was so intrigued by what I had shared with her, she started telling the other workers, about what I

The First Angel Visit

experienced. Before you knew it, we were all rejoicing and giving GOD PRAISE!

Wow, a visit from an Angel! Can't get any better than that! I was assured within myself, that GOD WAS GOING TO ALLOW ME TO LIVE!

Chapter 10

The California Hospital Visit

Living in Texas was absolutely refreshing. The kids and I was getting ready for our summer trip and someway, somehow as I mentioned before, our trip kept being extended. Fast forward after our summer trip, we went back to Texas. I was in the process of getting us another home, and right at the closing line, everything fell apart. The representation I had was not a good fit, or at least that's not how I conduct business, and once again we didn't have a solid place to stay. School was about to start, and I had no other choice. We must go back to California, I thought. My mom had been offering for quite some time now, and quite frankly, she didn't want us to leave after the summer was over! Well, I had to make the call and tell her we were coming back. Now it is much more complicated to decide to do something when you don't want to, or at least when you don't think it's something you want to do.

California bound, and by now, I would say, due to lack of treatment at this point, going from here, there, and everywhere, getting off my regimens, and all the sorts, my tumor was touching my collar bone! It had gotten so big. It was so noticeable, and every day I had to try to camouflage that it was there! It was an uncomfortable feeling, and I know how people feel who may not look normal feel. I was normal, I just had a distraction. It made me push harder, I remember shutting everything down, putting encouraging posts on Facebook. Meanwhile, people didn't really know those messages were to encourage me first! People didn't understand how much I was going through, and to top it off, it was ugly. I remember visiting with the Pastor and First Lady, and I told her it's just so ugly, and she said, "No, it's not!" The tumor will die! They prayed over me and I was still regaining strength and I kept thanking God for my HEALING! And I'm telling you I went deep with TOTAL RESTORATION, and WHOLENESS! Like the woman with the issue of blood, it was her faith that made her whole, remember that? So, there I was professing my faith daily, and praying constantly. Meanwhile, I wasn't feeling so well on the inside. My muscle mass was gone, and I was all bones. I was super small and super fragile! My family was concerned, but they didn't say much about it. I could fit size 6 clothes, and some 4's. Now you know that was too little for a girl my stature! Meanwhile, I kept smiling, I kept praying and I kept a positive mindset. IF

The California Hospital Visit

ANYONE came talking negative to me about my health, respectfully I had to SHUT IT DOWN! Now, about your own life, you must be careful what you ALLOW people to speak over your life! Words are POWERFUL! "Sticks and stones may break my bones, but words may never hurt me!" LIES! LIES! LIES! Yeah, I was guilty of saying that little saying too, until I gained WISDOM and experienced being lashed by people who took my lowest moments in life and turned my situation against me! Once you set hurtful words into the atmosphere, they can NEVER BE RETRACTED! God will not confirm anything to someone else before he has given it to YOU first! That's why the Bible says: to Study to show thy self-approved, that means you must know for yourself on how to discern when a person is given you HOG-WASH... REMEMBER THAT!

Study to show thyself approved unto GOD, a workman that needeth not to be ashamed, rightly dividing the word of truth. II Timothy 2:15 NKV

As time passed, we were considered settled in. My kids and I were staying with my mom, and things appeared to be getting normal. On the other hand, I was out one day, and I kept feeling like my shirt was wet. Imagine when you wash your hands and there are no towels to dry off, you wipe your hands on your shirt, and it has a somewhat damp feeling. Now I know I'm not the only who have done this at least once. My shirt felt wet. So, I looked at myself, only to see blood was coming through my shirt! Listen, anyone in my situation might have panicked, but I was trying to figure out what was my next move! My

The 2ⁿᵈ Time Around

mom was in Amsterdam, so I couldn't tell her. Now, my kids always tell me I have super POWERS, but I tell them it's the anointing. However, I knew that if I contacted my mom in AMSTERDAM, she would be home in five minutes. Not literally, but you get my drift.

Let's reminisce for a moment. When my husband passed away, which by now had been at least five years ago, I called my mom, she was working for Metropolitan Transit Authority at the time. She had just pulled her bus out for her route. Honestly, she wasn't supposed to pick up the phone, but I guess when your kids call in the wee hours of the morning, as a parent you answer! I told her that Hampton passed... I remember she said to me, "Shalana I'm so sorry. Let me pull this bus in," with nervousness in her voice and then said, "I will see you later." Now when a person passes away, its hours that go by. My husband had passed in the morning. After everything was said and done, the announcement, my pastor coming, the chaplain and pastor praying for me and my babies, my kids arriving to the hospital after it was officially announced that my husband was now pronounced deceased, explaining all that to my kids, crying in that closed-in room, that I felt was suffocating all of us at once, because literally our lives will be forever changed. ALL of that! Now, it's finally time to go home. We are leaving the hospital. When I got home, I didn't have a key, imagine that. I left in such a frantic, I had to ring my own doorbell. Ding dong, I rang it again, and there she was, my superhero! My mom, Pooch as many of you know her by, she opened the door. I couldn't take it

The California Hospital Visit

anymore, I couldn't believe that she was even there! I just fainted in her arms. LITERALLY! YEAH, these are the type of SUPER POWERS MOMS HAVE! I will NEVER FORGET HOW SHE MADE ME A PRIORITY and attended to us at one of the LOWEST points of my life! She was there, over 1400 miles away, by the time I got home from the hospital, she was there!

So back to her being in Amsterdam, I just knew I couldn't call, and besides, it was really nothing to worry about, right? Well, that's not necessarily true! I had to keep my cool. My mind was racing, what do I do? I can't go to the hospital, because who is going to take care of my babies? How are they going to get to school? So, I went to Target. I know, crazy, huh? I told the pharmacist what happened, he looked worried. I asked him was there anything he suggested I could put on the tumor cause now its bleeding, and I just moved here from Texas and our insurance hasn't transferred yet. He looked at me very concerned. His reply was that I needed to go to the hospital! Oh, my goodness! This can't be happening. I couldn't call my mom. I wasn't going to ruin her trip. I know how much it cost to go overseas, so I told my sisters, and I ended up at the hospital. They decided to keep me. I was there for five days and was told that I needed to go to a different hospital. The holidays were approaching and absolutely NO WAY was I going to do all of that during the holiday. I felt fine, I was just bleeding. At least that's what I kept telling myself. My worry was not really my health. I knew the enemy was mad. I was able to share my testimony in several parts of the globe,

The 2nd Time Around

so you best believe, he TRIED to get me to BELIEVE that God didn't HEAL me, but the DEVIL IS A LIE! I love saying that! My sisters helped me in ways I didn't know they could. They assured me daily that my kids were fine! Honestly, that was my main concern.

Chapter 11

After the Holidays

After the holidays were over, I had to mentally prepare myself to go back to the hospital that was suggested. I was now in a new facility, and HONEY when I tell you this one TRIED ME! I stayed in prayer. My goal was to GET OUT OF THERE, that was number one, and number two, get this tumor off of me! When the doctors would come check on me, I would say, "Are you guys going to do surgery?" My surgery request kept being declined, to the point that now the breast surgeon claimed the tumor was too big. They were AFRAID that if they took it, they would have to give me a skin graph, and take part of my back, to cover the wound. They were also afraid that it wouldn't heal properly because the areas were so stretched out. Wait a minute! *For God hath not given us the spirit of fear; but of Power, and of Love, and of a sound mind.* I felt the chaos and confusion, and God just does not operate like that. Mentally it was tough, there were oncology doctors, breast surgeons, regular doctors, all who would see me daily. I had test on top of test, on top of x-rays and exams, on top of MRI's, CTSCAN's, you name it! All these things were happening, yet I couldn't seem to hear from one doctor who had the confidence to tackle this thing. I stayed in my word, and I kept referencing the scriptures of healing! HEALING, it still exists. HEALING can happen!

Mentally, I was worn out in the natural, but I had to keep my spirit refueled. I had one doctor come and talk to me. She told me, "We are going to have to start chemo, because the tumor was too big, and we can't do surgery that size," and on and on! Well you know my mind is racing in disbelief. I've seen shows where twins were separated and able to live. I heard of people who had brain tumors and are still living to this day. I've heard of testimonies where people were only given a little time to live, and they are still ALIVE today. I'm sorry, but YOU CAN'T TELL ME WHAT GOD CAN'T DO! I've tried him for myself and I know HE CAN DO ANYTHING BUT FAIL! Come on now! "Shalana, are you listening? Shalana, honey, did you hear me?" When I came to myself. I said, "Yes, I heard you!" This doctor was very aggressive, and I could tell she was so convincing that she more than likely hasn't experienced someone challenging her! I looked at her, and I sat up in the bed, and now I guess this is where I had to use my HOLY GHOST BOLDNESS! I said "Ma'am, with all due respect, that's not something that I'm willing to do." She said, "Well, you have no other choice!" I said, "Sure I do. There are a ton of choices!" Side note: don't EVER allow someone to

After the Holidays

pin you in a corner and make you feel like you have to make a decision that you know in your heart you don't agree with. "Shalana, what is it? Why don't you want to take the chemo? Chemo helps people to live. Chemo will help you get better." I said, "Ma'am, I'm not doing that!" The other doctor took her outside the curtain. He was talking low and I couldn't hear him, but it didn't matter because my mind was made up! She came back in the room, and she said, "Honey, listen, I'm sorry about your husband and I'm sorry you had to go through all of this. But if you agree to take the chemo we MIGHT (well see that's where she really messed up) be able to shrink the tumor. Then we can do the surgery and get you all better." "Ma'am, I'm not doing that!" Ohhhhhhhhhh boy when the enemy gets stirred up, I'm telling you, they will go for the jugular. And that doctor said to me verbatim, "If you don't take the CHEMO, you might as well prepare your kids to live with someone else, pack them up, because you WILL DIE!" OHHHHHHHHH NOOOOO SHE DIDN'T! No, ma'am! This woman struck a nerve! See when you're saved, you don't have to cuss and act a fool, but you can shut someone down with the WORD OF GOD! I told that lady boldly, "I REBUKE THAT STATEMENT. God said I SHALL LIVE and NOT DIE and you can't give me an expiration date! I'm really not taking it now! The room is starting to spin, you are working up my anxiety, and I NEED YOU TO EXCUSE YOURSELF!"

Then she tried to get all educational on me. Don't get it twisted, I have a MASTER'S degree, but to some people they could care less about your accolades. I have the funniest story: my Coach Terence Smith, one day was talking to someone who tried to throw their education on him. The woman was talking about all her degrees and that she graduated Magnum cum laude, and my Coach responded, LADDIE DODDIE! I laugh every time I hear him say that, He always say he has a GED, which is a GOOD ENOUGH DEGREE! So, in other words, he's made millions without the degrees, and the lady, well, you get my point!

THE ONCOLOGIST PROCEEDED TO SAY, "If you TRUST IN YOUR GOD (ohhh boy she's really trying me now! My GOD? Hmmmm, well that let me know we are on two different pages!) If you trust in your GOD, you will trust the fact that He has us in position to be doctors and make decisions." I said, "Yes, I agree. But God does not operate in confusion and I've already told you what I wasn't doing. And besides *you* haven't given me any other alternative other than chemo." Which I know by now she didn't read my previous reports, because clearly it will tell you that I don't have that TYPE that requires CHEMO! See what I mean? There are times in life when you feel like you have no other choice, but to go with what you know in your heart is not right! Now let me be the first one to say, anyone who have taken chemo, that's their choice. My comments, thoughts, and feelings are personal. I don't down play anyone who chooses to do it. However, for more reasons than not, that's not my story, and that's not my testimony.

By this time, I had really tuned this woman out. Why was she still talking to me? LORD, I don't want to be rude,

After the Holidays

make her leave NOW! Good grief. Leave me alone! "I already told you I wasn't doing that, so either we can come up with another option, but I have a headache now, and I'm ready to go to sleep." This woman was furious with me! But guess what? She didn't stop there, she kept going! Then she sat even closer, she said, "Let me tell you a story!" I have my eyes closed, and although she was a beautiful lady, I was sick of looking at her! Anyway, she proceeded with her story. She said, "A person gets into a situation, and they ask God for help. God sends the helicopter, they didn't take it. They said, 'No thank you, I'm waiting on GOD!' A little while later, the person is asking God for help, and then they see a boat..." I knew in the back of my mind I heard this story before, but she was kind of mixing it around. She continued, "Then the person goes, 'No thank you, I'm waiting for God.'" I don't remember what the third help was, because like I said I had TUNED HER OUT. She continued on, "but then the person passed away. When they got to Heaven, they said to God, 'I asked you for help and you let me die', and God said, 'I sent it. I sent a helicopter, a boat, etc. and you didn't take it.' The moral of the story is, we are your help and if you don't take it, then you know what's going to happen! I would hate to see that happen to you!" Wait a minute, I thought. Did she just indirectly tell me again I would die if I didn't do what she said? "Okay, that's it," I replied, "I've HAD ENOUGH! GET OUT OF MY ROOM! LEAVE ME ALONE! You are taking this wayyyyyyyyy too far!" Now let me tell you something, the enemy always know how to dress up and look attractive! I really told this lady that what she just said to me was a story we used in business (to help others believe in their business model and concepts), and that NO WHERE was that story in the WORD OF GOD! "Now, if you'd like to prove me wrong, I will sit here." I said as I'm handing her my bible. "I will sit here and let you show me where I missed that scripture." Honey, if looks could kill! She had nothing else to say, and you know what? She said, "I WILL LEAVE YOU ALONE!" That's what I thought! Lights out! Lord, this woman really tried me!

Prior to the oncologist leaving my room, I was given some medicine. I really don't know what it was, but I needed her and that experience out of its misery! I got as comfortable as I could and went to sleep! Finally, lights out!

Upon all this stuff happening, God showed me the tumor. It was significantly smaller and in my breast area where it was, my skin was almost like a milk chocolate color. That's because of how large it stretched itself out of shape and discolored. Once it died out, I saw a quick glimpse of it being gone. So according to what the doctors were saying, it was going against everything that GOD showed me! So, I knew someway somehow, this thing was leaving my body.

When I woke up, there were two small little men in my room! These men were so short, they reminded me of dwarfs. They were as tall as a smurf. Hopefully, you've seen that cartoon. Anyway, one of them had a clipboard, and both of their backs were facing me! When they realized I was awake, they both turned around and

After the Holidays

smiled! The one with the clip board said, "YAYYYYYY your surgery has been approved." I just looked at him. He smiled again and said, "Your surgery, it's been approved." While looking at the clipboard you couldn't make out the words. It was like how they do it on cartoons with lines going down the paper. I have very good vison, but I couldn't make out anything. I was really tripping, because these guys were so little! Where did they come from? When the one with the clipboard said, "Your surgery have been approved." The other one started dancing moving his hands up and down cheering for me! Gosh, these guys had the biggest smiles! Then I jumped up! Huh? The room was pitch dark. I was asleep. Was it angels? Well, needless to say, exactly what the vision showed me about the tumor, IT happened! I didn't have surgery, but in terms of the saying, "God will be your physician," man as time passed, I got myself out that hospital and before I knew it, I looked up and that tumor was GONE! Once again, and like I said before, you can't tell me what GOD CAN'T DO! There is NOTHING TOO HARD FOR GOD!

Chapter 12

The Healing Zone!

Shhhhhh!!! In order for the body to heal, you MUST REST! Rest in your mind, body and spirit. If the body is (un)eased, it then can become DISEASED. This can contribute to tragedies, unfortunate occurrences in one's life, heartbreak, depression, just to name a few. You are what you THINK about it! If you are consistently feeding into the negative occurrences, as opposed to thinking of the positive outcome, then unfortunately you will attract the negative. I have learned over the years, if you give the body what it needs, it will give you what you need; optimal health is obtainable.

In terms of healing, there are so many circumstances to which this applies. You don't have to be diagnosed specifically with cancer to need healing. There are things that you might have endured, that you need to be HEALED FROM! It's not always a case of a sickness per say, but there are all sorts of things that can require healing. Unforgiveness, hatred, jealousy, back stabbing, hurting people intentionally, gossiping, rage, depression, demonic attacks, should I go on? You get the point.

One of my hardest HEALING OCCURANCES: when my husband fell and busted his head open, I faulted myself for years, why didn't I hear him get up? If only I had heard him, he would have never fell. Did I do everything as a wife to save his life? What if I gave him more product that I knew was killing off the tumor? Should I have changed the little bit of diet he had? On and on and on! I was so hard on myself. We all have an expiration date, but only God knows it! So that day was Hampton's request that I believe was granted for him to go home (Heaven). It didn't matter if I did feel him get up, at some part during that day, at that specific time, he would have passed. So, I had to heal from BLAMING myself for the circumstance in which I had no control over!

Secondly, before walking out of the house, I asked my son to please put a towel over the pool of blood in the kitchen! I was crying so hard, come to find out, he misunderstood what I said. When I got home from the hospital, the pool of blood was gone! My house was full of people. I was crying so hard I couldn't even get the words out! I didn't mean any harm, I just didn't want my girls to wake up and see the pool of blood in the kitchen. To even think that it was so gruesome, I didn't want my girls to be devastated. Hampton's passing was more than enough. So, my request was, "Son, please put a towel over the blood!"

The Healing Zone!

"Tyion, where is the blood?" I asked. He said, "Mom, I cleaned it up like you told me!" Honestly, I wanted to DIE! It felt like my heart was ripped out of my chest. His eyes welled up with tears, and I said, "NOOOOOO, son," crying so hard, "I just wanted you to cover it! You cleaned it up by yourself?" "Yes," He replied. "Tyion, I am so sorry!" I was immediately sick to my stomach. I wanted to vomit. Just at the thought, that my son, who was only twelve at the time. I'm sure he was so traumatized. The thought was killing me! I carried that weight for years. I kept having flashbacks of him on the floor, and how he would be tormented for years! This was a heavy, heavy weight! I cried over this situation all the time. I felt like a bad mom. And you know what? All the while it was a misunderstanding! The thought, the blood, the TORMENT! "Tyion, Mommy is so sorry!" I've apologized to him several times. He said, "Mom, it's okay." But honestly, I felt horrible behind the whole thing. So, this one of the main things, I had to FORGIVE MYSLEF! Forgiveness of self is a sign of HEALING! If you don't FORGIVE yourself, YOU CAN'T HEAL! I love you son, and once again, I am truly sorry for the misunderstanding of instructions.

The Healing Zone has been an eight-year journey since I was diagnosed with breast cancer! I'm still alive, and although things are not perfect, God is perfecting me in His own image! He gave me a 2nd Chance to LIVE! Truthfully, more chances than that! I've experienced miracle after miracle in regard to my healing. The assignment on my life should have wiped me out! I have

The 2nd Time Around

held on to God's promises even when I couldn't see my way to health. I have pressed through pain that has been so excruciating, I thought I wasn't going to make it (yes, the pain was that bad). There have been times when I've literally only had the size of a mustard seed to hold on to (trust me, the actual seed itself is very tiny), because I really didn't know the outcome! All I knew was that I trust GOD!

This book was to encourage you and inspire you to become better. Seek your purpose, align yourself with individuals who have what you desire. Seek God diligently, and he will give you the desires of your heart!

My FIRST favorite gospel artist is Shirley Cesar. I love her because she is so anointed. I listened to her as a young girl and I wanted to model after her. I wanted her anointing, because I know she was the real deal! One of her songs, she said YOU are NEXT IN LINE for a MIRACLE! Now I don't know exactly what you are or have been seeking God for, but I do know that if you APPLY the teachings, you will come out victorious! I know if you JUST DO THE WORK and not worry about HOW you are going to get things done, God can BLESS YOU! I also know that if you move yourself out of the way, He will order your steps. Sometimes we get into our own way and block our destiny. If you are hanging around people with no purpose, change your circle! Yep, I said it. You must be BOLD and strong, to not get distracted by the distractions. Remember this, every good thing is not the GOD thing. If it's not ordained by God, you shouldn't want ANY part of it!

The Healing Zone!

Shirley Cesar, said, "A Miracle is: A supernatural gift that only God can give!" MIRACLES ARE STILL VERY PREVALENT IN TODAY'S TIME! Don't give up on the things God has promised you! If He said it, it will come to pass!

My faith in KNOWING, BELIEVING, AND PERSERVERING became powerful! All the things I endured, I KNOW it was nobody but GOD! The fact that I'm in my right state of mind, and have you heard the saying, 'Thank God I don't look like what I've been through!" Faith in BELIEVING that GOD can do the IMPOSSIBLE! In my journey, it didn't matter what the situation looked like. I had faith to BELIEVE that all things are possible to those that believe, and faith in prospering! I've always been blessed, even in my lowest of low. God will supply all your needs according to HIS RICHES and GLORY! I knew I had complete access to change my situation. I learned if it was going to be, then it was up to me! I took my journey seriously, I knew that I was to remind God's people that HE STILL HEALS! And I promised, if He let me live, I will impact millions of people all across the world! MY TESTIMONY will WOW THE PEOPLE!—Elder Anthony Bernard Hampton. Well, you are reading about a miracle, about a woman who desires to impact millions through her testimony who had every VALID reason to throw in the towel! God allowed me to LIVE for this moment right now and to help PUSH you to your purpose!

The 2nd Time Around

If I walk the walk, I have to talk the talk. In other words, practice what you preach! EAT CLEAN, exercise, even if you just take a daily walk, detox your body (there are so many juicing components you can try), GET PLENTY OF SLEEP! Stay hydrated and DRINK PLENTY of WATER! REST, that means some days you have to slow down and not do much of anything! HAVE SOME ME TIME! Practice SELF LOVE and reward yourself for accomplishments. SET your AFFIRMATIONS FOR what you want to accomplish. Set long term and short-term goals, because if it's a dream and there's no plan, then it's just a dream! Set your goals so high that they scare you! I learned all these things doing personal development over the years. I learned from the best. Years and years of gold nuggets and tools in which I have to apply for my own life! I had to read some of the material more than once. GET OUT of your own way and GET TO WORK! SO THAT YOUR BODY CAN HEAL, start juicing, take your supplements, watch labels when you are shopping.

Lastly, I will leave you with this... you must learn to PUSH through the PAIN! P—PUSH, through every adversity that comes your way, A—Activate your actions and DO THE WORK, I—BE INSPIRED, and N—never ever ever quit!

My latter days will be better than my former. My LIFE is not over, it's just STARTING! This is my eighth year of surviving, and in biblical terms, the number eight symbolizes NEW BEGINNINGS! I'm so thankful GOD

The Healing Zone!

ALLOWED ME TO LIVE! I'm ready to WALK in the ABUNDANCE OF OVERFLOW! God will CONTINUE to get the glory out of my life, ohhh and don't forget... it's okay to be saved and be WEALTHY!

BELIEF + FAITH = MIRACLES! Ladies and Gentlemen, YOU ARE NEXT IN LINE FOR YOUR MIRACLE! DO YOU BELIVE IT? I had to write this book as if my life depended on it. You know WHY? Because it did! It's not about me, but it's about you. BELIEVE AGAIN, DREAM AGAIN, RESET YOUR GOALS, and APPLY what you have been given! God Bess you!

REFERENCES

1. Hill, Napoleon. <u>Think and Grow Rich</u>, Forgotten Books, 2008

2. World Bible Publishers, Inc. <u>Holy Bible</u>, New King James Version, 1909 Edition, The Scofield Reference Bible.

3. RIFETECH Article, Dr. Royal RIFE

4. Eckhardt, John. Prayers that move Mountains, 2012

5. Dickerman, Don. <u>When Pigs Move in,</u> 2009

www.ingramcontent.com/pod-product-compliance
Lightning Source LLC
Chambersburg PA
CBHW050651160426
43194CB00010B/1896